322.4
ALI   Alibrandi, Tom
       Hate is my neighbor

DATE DUE

Also by Tom Alibrandi

Non-Fiction

Free Yourself
The Meditation Handbook
Biorhythms: Get The Most Out Of Your Life
Young Alcoholics
Privileged Information (with Frank Armani)

Poetry

Hallways, Poems of Transition

Fiction

Killshot
Uncle Joe Shannon (novelization of a screenplay by Burt Young)
Custody
Burnout
Blood Fortunes

Published by Stand Together Publishers
P.O. Box 425
Ellensburg, WA 98926-0425

Library of Congress Catalogue #99-072865
Current Affairs

ISBN #0-9674044-0-1

Cover Art, copyright © Mary Frances
Cover Design by Susan Burghart
Tom Alibrandi photo by Peter Brown
Bill Wassmuth photo by Chris Nordfors

Acknowledgments

Without Bill Wassmuth's help and ongoing belief in the project, this book would not have been written. I am also thankful to the members of the Kootenai County Task Force on Human Relations who gave generously of their time and energy.

I am grateful to my brother, Michael, for his continuing affirmation of my work. And to my father, John, for teaching me to think critically and to hang in there.

Last but certainly not least, I thank my son, Sabin. If he is representative of the new generation, I know it will be free of much of the race hatred and intolerance perpetuated by my generation, and by those that came before.

Tom Alibrandi

Tom Alibrandi is the initiator and visionary behind this book. A creative man of great energy, he transformed thousands of pieces of information into a literary work that gives this true story permanence. I am grateful to be Tom's partner in this project, as well as his friend.

I acknowledge with great respect the real heroes of this story, the members of the Kootenai County Task Force on Human Relations. They, and all the good people of the Coeur d'Alene area, have for two decades continued the fight against the evil of racism; we are a better country because of their courageous actions.

The people of St. Pius Parish have supported me through many challenging times. They will never fully know the impact that they have on my life. Without them, there would be no story to tell. I am very grateful.

Bill Wassmuth

Dedication

I dedicate this book with all my love to my favorite Swedish redhead.

TA

For my parents, models of respect and hard work, and in memory of Sam Stone.

BW

All hybrids called Jews are to be repatriated from the Republic's territory, all their wealth be redistributed to restore our people, and it shall be a capital offense to advocate or promote Jew Talmudic anti-Christ Communism in any manner or any other crimes against nature.

Richard Butler

ONE

1980

Not yet nine o'clock, it was already warm. Today promised to be hot and humid, with bloated cumulus clouds rolling in from the West, weather that reminded Sid Rosen of his native St. Paul, Minnesota. The sixty-three year old Rosen lived in St. Paul until he was twenty, when he joined the Air Force during World War II. At the completion of his four year tour of duty, Rosen moved to north Idaho, where his parents had relocated during the war.

Rosen immediately fell in love with the unspoiled beauty of north Idaho. He worked as a bartender in local restaurants, until he opened his own place, a steak and ribs joint in Hayden Lake.

He eased his blue Chevrolet into an empty spot in front of the Post Office. He stepped out of his car.

A deceptively strong man, despite his lean build, with a bush of dark hair and sapphire-colored eyes, Rosen entered the Post Office. He waved to the Postmaster, before opening his mailbox. He withdrew a stack of letters, and thumbed through the mail like a blackjack dealer fanning a deck of cards. Most of it was bills; there was a letter from Temple Beth Shalom in Spokane.

Rosen opened the envelope from the Temple, and read as he walked out of the Post Office. It was an invitation to a steering committee meeting about the upcoming Holocaust commemoration ceremony.

Rosen returned the letter to the envelope, and reached through the open window of his car and dropped the batch of mail on the front seat. Doing so, he made a mental note to attend the meeting at the Temple in Spokane, 30 miles west of Hayden Lake. There was only a handful of Jews in north Idaho, and those, like Sid Rosen, who practiced their faith had to drive to Spokane to do it. For Rosen, the sense of community and comfort the congregation provided him had become even more important in the past eight years, since his wife, Dolores, passed away from cancer. His friends at Temple Beth Shalom helped him feel less isolated.

Rosen pushed into the front door of the Owl Café, located next door to the Post Office. The several tables were occupied, so Sid took a seat at the counter.

"Good morning, Sid. What'll it be?" the thin waitress in the starched, sand-colored uniform inquired.

"Two eggs, basted, home fries, and whole wheat toast," he answered.

"Orange juice, and coffee?" she queried.

"Please," he finished.

She wrote his order on her pad, tore off the top sheet, and clipped it on the carousal on the shelf of the pass window between the counter area and kitchen.

Rosen watched as the waitress poured him a cup of coffee. He added a splash of milk, stirred, and took a sip. While drinking his coffee, he allowed his mind to slip into gear, and, like a car engine beginning a gradual ascent up a steep hill from a dead start, his thoughts turned over slowly.

Business at his restaurant had been slow lately, what with the closing of the silver mines in nearby Kellogg. The loss of jobs meant economic hard times, and the first thing people cut out when money got tight was eating out at restaurants. Then there were the difficulties of raising four children alone. Despite his having been blessed with almost indefatigable endurance, being a single parent and running a business was at times more than he could handle. His daily ritual of having breakfast at the Owl Café was one of the few breaks he got between six in the morning, when he awakened, until one a.m., the time he arrived home after closing the restaurant. He hired a woman to help him at home with the cooking and cleaning, but he was still on the go almost 20 hours a day.

The waitress placed his order in front of him. The smell of eggs and potatoes turned his thoughts to satisfying his hunger. He focused on his food, and began eating.

Rosen was about halfway through his breakfast, when loud laughter from the table in the far corner of the café caught his attention. He turned to see five men sitting around the table, coffee cups and empty plates in front of them. Rosen recognized the guy with the hard, dark eyes and neatly combed salt-and-pepper hair, wearing his customary pale blue, starched shirt with the red and blue patch on each shoulder. It was Richard Butler, Minister of the Church of Jesus Christ Christian, whose headquarters was located about two minutes from Rosen's 25 acre farm. Though they knew one another, the two men had never spoken. Butler was the leader of the Aryan Nations movement, a group whose avowed purpose was to turn north Idaho into an all-white, Christian homeland. Butler and

Rosen, therefore, were sworn enemies.

Butler turned to Rosen, and their eyes met for a second. A hint of a smile played at Butler's lips.

To hell with him, Rosen thought, and turned away.

Those Aryan jerks could think or say or believe anything they wanted as long as they left him alone; he was not going to let them intimidate him. As far as he was concerned they were a bunch of room-temperature-IQ loonies.

Rosen finished his breakfast and paid his bill. He pushed off the stool, and turned for the front door. He paused a moment when he heard someone utter his name. He turned and looked. No one acknowledged his eyes. Rosen shrugged his shoulders and left the Owl Café.

He climbed into his car and drove around the corner to his restaurant. Once the building came into sight, he slowed his car. Painted on the rough-hewn, weathered planks across the front wall of his restaurant—in white, letters about three feet tall—was, "Jewswine" and "KKK." Between the slur and the KKK logo was a swastika.

Rosen stopped his car, and slammed the transmission into park. He sat there for a moment, while the ball of bitter rage rose from his stomach into his throat.

"Lousy Aryan bastards," he mouthed.

TWO

The heavy-set, sad-faced Larry Broadbent steered his unmarked brown Buick along Highway 95, the road to Sandpoint, and eventually Canada. Broadbent turned off Highway 95, to Hayden Avenue. He was on his way to Hayden Lake for a meeting called by a group of locals to discuss the defacing of Sid Rosen's Restaurant.

Broadbent lit a cigarette, and drew deeply on it. Exhaling a shaft of smoke, he glanced ruefully at the smoldering cigarette. He was already into his second pack of the day and the hands had not met at the top of the clock. Someday, he promised, he would chuck this habit, one he had been trying for years to break. God only knew how his wife and kids had been after him to quit.

Absentmindedly steering his car along the road towards the Wedgwood-blue lake, Broadbent caught himself staring about like a tourist. He smiled to himself. This was sure beautiful country. Living in Kootenai County a little more than a month, he still felt as if he was on vacation. Broadbent had come to this north Idaho hill country from Burley in southern Idaho, where the landscape was parched and flat and practically devoid of trees. He had been chief of police of Burley; before that, he had served in the State's Attorney General's office. Broadbent had been talked into moving north by Merf Stalder, recently elected Kootenai County Sheriff. Broadbent jumped at the chance. Besides the opportunity to live in north Idaho, he was excited about serving with Stalder; both men came out of the old school of law enforcement, and Broadbent had correctly figured they would work well together.

Broadbent eased his Buick to a stop in front of Sid Rosen's restaurant. It had been nearly a week since Rosen had reported the incident, the anti-Semitic slurs were still scrawled across the front wall. Broadbent paused a moment before opening his car door. For the life of him he could not figure out why Merf Stalder had asked him, of all people, to join him out here for this meeting. Broadbent figured he was the last guy to represent the Sheriff's Department in matters dealing with racism, bigotry, or anti-Semitism. Raised in predominantly white Weiser, a town of about 3000 in southwestern Idaho, Broadbent could not even remember if there had been any Jewish people in his hometown. The only minorities he encountered while growing up were Mexican migrant workers who came through in the summer to harvest the crops. Broadbent had never been involved in any civil rights activities, nor as a law enforcement officer in Idaho had much occasion to come face to face with discrimination. Civil rights, human rights and discrimination were issues Larry Broadbent had heard about on television. That stuff happened in the South and in big cities, not in Idaho, with its minuscule population of people of color.

Broadbent pushed out of his car. He buttoned his blue suit jacket, hiding the Colt .38 Detective Special in his shoulder holster, and obscuring his generous paunch.

Here goes nothing, he thought as he flipped his cigarette into a nearby puddle, where it died with a hiss. He cinched up his pants, and stepped through the front door of the restaurant.

Broadbent ran his eyelids up and down a couple of times over his moist, hazel eyes to help them adjust to the shadowed interior. He got his bearings and noted the group sitting around the table in the middle of the dining room. He recognized the woman at the head of the table as Dina Tanners, a dark-haired, petite and attractive Jewish woman. Tanners had piercing dark eyes, and the habit of talking in quick, short bursts, like corn coming to a pop. She was an extremely serious woman, and was known around the area as a civil rights activist.

Those sitting around the table noticed Broadbent, and several of them stood to greet the Undersheriff-elect as he approached the table.

Sid Rosen stepped over to Broadbent.

"You are?" Rosen asked.

"Undersheriff Larry Broadbent."

The restaurant owner ran his hand down the front of his white shirt in a futile attempt to press the wrinkles out of the cotton. Rosen looked as though he had slept in his clothes.

"Glad you could make it," Rosen added.

Rosen's guarded expression puzzled the police officer. Broadbent felt the man's reaction was a bit overdone for the amount of damage done to his building.

"Come, sit," Sid Rosen said, graciously. "I'll get you a cup of coffee."

Rosen padded over to the nearby waitress station to pour Broadbent a cup of coffee from the pot sitting on the warmer. The police officer took turns greeting everyone at the table.

Sheriff Merf Stalder, a stout, disheveled-looking man, who appeared as though he would be more at home on a tractor than in a police cruiser, nodded to Broadbent from the other end of the table. Stalder was anything but the traditional spit-and-polish police officer, something the Undersheriff liked.

"Merf," Broadbent answered.

Glen Walker, incoming Kootenai County prosecutor, took Broadbent's hand.

"Larry, I'd like you to meet these people," the intense, wiry, olive-skinned Walker announced.

"This is Marshall Mend," Glen Walker said.

The balding, broad-faced Marshall Mend leaned across the table with a style and intensity that reminded Broadbent of a fighter moving in to throw a body shot.

"Nice to meet you," Mend said. The real estate man had an alert, muscular body, and a salesperson's charm.

"You, too," Broadbent responded.

"I'm Rick Morse," the short, bearded, slightly built man to Broadbent's right said.

The Undersheriff took Morse's soft, pink hand. Morse was a Protestant Minister, who, along with Bill Wassmuth, pastor of St. Pius Catholic Church, was known around town as a leading social activist.

The Undersheriff took turns greeting Bill Brown, an attorney; David Cohen, a Sociology Instructor at North Idaho College in Coeur d'Alene; Dina Tanners; and Mel Starr, a local businessman.

Sid Rosen returned to the table. He placed a mug of coffee in front of the Undersheriff. Broadbent took a sip of the hot, bitter coffee, and added sugar.

"To bring you up to speed, Larry," Glen Walker explained, "we'd just been discussing the implications of the defacing of Sid's restaurant."

"In addition," Merf Stalder added, "we've been given information that Mr. Rosen has been followed by certain persons."

Broadbent scratched his chin. Merf must have just learned about Rosen being followed, since they had talked the previous evening and the Sheriff had not mentioned it.

The Undersheriff glanced at Rosen. On the Jewish man's chiseled face was the hunted, terrorized look Broadbent had seen on men who knew their lives were in danger.

"Without knowing who wrote those things on the building, or who might be following Sid," Walker picked up, "we can only speculate why these things are being done."

David Cohen leaned his forearms on the wooden table. He wrapped his hands around his coffee mug as he was trying to turn it into powder.

"Excuse me, Glen," the short, wiry, and balding Cohen cut in. "But I don't think any one of us in this room has any doubt who wrote that garbage on Sid's restaurant, or who might be tailing him. And 'why' the Aryans did it is self-evident; they're harassing Sid because of his faith."

Walker pushed his quill-like brown hair off his forehead. Broadbent had pegged Walker as a patient man, whose will could turn to iron when he knew he was right about something.

"We don't know for sure if the Aryans did it," Walker put in. "Let's give Merf Stalder and his people time to come up with something."

The mention of the word Aryans caused Larry Broadbent's ears to open up like microwave receptors. The last time the Undersheriff had heard that term was in the context of World War II.

"I don't know how much more clearly these people could telegraph their actions," Dina Tanners countered. She slid a sheath of papers down the table, towards the county prosecutor. "Father Bill Wassmuth gave me these."

Walker glanced down at the flyers and pamphlets.

"I know about this trash," Walker said. "It's nothing. These people are pathetic, comical fools."

Larry Broadbent picked up one of the pamphlets. On the cover was a red and blue shield, superimposed over which was the letter 'N', bisected by a vertical crown-topped sword. The pamphlet was entitled, "ARYAN NATIONS, THE CHURCH OF JESUS CHRIST CHRISTIAN DOCTRINE OF FAITH."

The Undersheriff leafed through the pages. He had never seen anything like this. Listed were thirty-four points claiming that Aryan people were the chosen people of God, divinely selected to lead all other races, and that this master race of whites was in danger of being overwhelmed by the sheer numbers of people of color. What Aryans that remained were slowly but surely being financially strangled and impoverished by the "Jew-run banking institutions and Zionist Occupied U.S. Government." According to the Aryan Nations' literature, this dwindling pool of Aryans was also rapidly becoming polluted because of intermarriage between whites and people of color. This consorting with non-whites, according to the document, was called miscegeny, a capital crime punishable by death. Further, in order to protect their race, the Aryans wished to transform the Pacific Northwest into a separate white nation, in which no people of color, Jews, homosexuals, nor mixed-race people could live, or even pass through.

Broadbent's eyes widened as he read.

"WE DEMAND: that citizenship in this whites-only homeland be limited to the Christian ARYAN RACE. Your race is your nation. Those Aryans entering our nation should not receive the citizenship until they have been here for three generations.

"A non-Aryan person or mixed race shall not be granted citizenship. We shall have no hyphenated citizens such as German-Americans, Mexican-Americans, Italian-Americans, Japanese-Americans or Chinese-Americans in our Christian country. All non-Aryans shall not enter this land. All found within our borders shall be utterly destroyed."

Broadbent had trouble comprehending that there were people who actually believed this stuff. He glanced through a few other points from the Aryans' Doctrine of Faith.

"We believe in the abolition of the federal progressive income tax and the disbanding of the 'Internal Revenue Service Jewocracy.'

"We believe in the abolition of the alien private Jewish controlled Federal Reserve System, to be replaced by control issuance of United States real money, interest free; that wealth is production, and speculation is Jewish rape of true producers.'

"We believe the Jews through their controlled media have successfully promoted birth control through abortion, the pill, and deliberate thwarting of childbirth by a multitude of means.'

"We believe in the immediate stopping of payment of money by Germany to Jews in Israel and all over the world for the alleged crimes Germany DID NOT COMMIT. A thorough accounting of all money forcefully extracted from Germany should be established and the Jews worldwide be made to repay with interest.

"We believe monopolies, chain stores, conglomerates and corporate farms violate God's Law. Monopolies bring a disproportionate share of the wealth under the control of Jews which kills Competition and the Private Enterprise system.

"We believe we must return back to the dietary and health laws of Scriptures and do away with junk and foodless foods, most of which are Kosher, or Jewish garbage.

"We believe in Aryan self-defense and the right of Aryans to keep and bear arms for the protection of their family and property from non-Aryan mamzers (bastard Hebrews)."

Broadbent slowly shook his head. This brand of hate was new to him.

He reached for one of the flyers. The red and blue Aryan swastika blazed across the top of the single sheet of white paper. Underneath was a poorly drawn silhouette of a black person, who appeared to be running. The caption read, "Come to the second annual Aryan Congress this summer. Paramilitary training, with the possibility of live nigger, Jew, Mexican and Gook targets."

Broadbent swallowed hard, then glanced up from the flyer. His eyes met Sid Rosen's for a brief moment. Rosen's expression seemed to be pleading with him to understand how he as a Jew felt about all of this.

"You may think these Aryans are a bunch of pathetic, comical fools," David Cohen explained to Glen Walker, "but we know better. We've seen this movie before."

"If you hadn't realized it by now, Glen, five of the eight private citizens here are Jewish," he added.

"You could say," Dina Tanners picked up, "that centuries of being persecuted—the Holocaust being just one of several periods throughout history in which millions of my people were killed—for no other reason than being Jewish, has provided us with an excellent early warning detection system against anti-Semitism."

"We have an inner antenna that picks up this kind of hate," David Cohen seconded, his lips fixed into a tight hard smile.

Larry Broadbent thought of the image of the canary in the mine shaft. He considered the sad reality that the canary had to die before it was determined that there was poisonous gas in the shaft.

"Aren't we getting a little strong about this?" Walker asked. "I really don't mean to downplay this incident, but after all aren't we just talking about some distasteful graffiti on the wall of this building? Or the possibility that someone might have followed Sid a couple of times?"

"What we're saying, Glen, and we hope you can hear this," Dina Tanners explained, with a hint of impatience, "is that what is written on the wall of this restaurant, and the fact that someone has been following Sid, signifies something more than that. Specifically, whomever painted those anti-Semitic slurs—and I have no doubt who did it—has made a bold public statement."

"It also shouldn't be forgotten," David Cohen added, "that people in Germany in the 1930's didn't take the Nazis seriously at first. They didn't realize the implications of the anti-Semitic slogans that began appearing on building walls and sidewalks all over Germany until it was too late."

Glen Walker nodded. He seemed to be conceding that he, as a Christian, could not understand the paranoia felt by Mend, Tanners, Cohen, Rosen and the other Jews in the room.

Larry Broadbent tried to work it around in his head that what was written on the front of Sid Rosen's building—along with the tail-job on Sid—was something more than a prank committed by an isolated person, some nut-case taking out his frustrations and venting his prejudices by scapegoating a Jewish businessman. Hell, it could even have been an enraged former employee of Rosen's.

Rick Morse tugged at his beard and leaned forward. In his thirties, thin in an unathletic, undeveloped sort of way, and wearing large brown-tinted glasses, Morse was seen as an ally of the progressive faction of Coeur d'Alene. Among conservatives he was privately referred to as a bleeding-heart liberal. He was pastor of the First Christian Church of Coeur d'Alene, and as president of the area's Ecumenical Association he was one of the more visible members of the clerical community, though not the most powerful nor influential.

"I think whomever spray-painted Sid's restaurant, or is following him, needs to understand that the community will not tolerate or support this sort of bigotry and prejudice," Morse began. He played with his beard, a scraggly, anarchistic bush of red that seemed incapable of prospering above his lip, where it tapered off into an early-adolescent downy fuzz. "It seems to me that we need to issue some kind of public statement that makes it clear that all of us in the community stand behind our Jewish brothers and sisters, as well as supporting the rights of blacks, Native Americans, and other minorities."

Broadbent found himself resisting what Morse said. From the old school, Larry Broadbent was still somewhat put off by long-haired, bearded, peacenik types.

"Are you talking about another statement, similar to the one the Ecumenical Association issued last year, in which you condemned the Aryans?" Walker asked.

"I'm not accusing Butler or the Aryans of what happened to Sid's restaurant, though Butler's people advocate racism and violence," Morse explained. "What I am suggesting is that the community come together in some way so that we send out a clear message that racism, bigotry and anti-Semitism are not going to be tolerated in this area. So far we've done nothing to counteract Butler's steady stream of rhetoric espousing his belief in white supremacy."

Morse paused, as if letting what he had just said sink in. "What particularly enrages me," he continued, "is that Butler has been using the name of Jesus Christ to advance his hate rhetoric. People in the community have been wondering why the ministers and the community leaders aren't doing anything to counteract what the Aryans are putting out."

"How do you figure to bring the community together?" Dina Tanners asked.

"I'm not sure," Morse explained. He went back to playing with his beard, and looked up, as if searching the ceiling for the answer. "I think I should contact pastors like Bill Wassmuth, and call a meeting of the Ecumenical Association. That way we can get this out in the open. All the area's clergy can have some input, and we can take a position as a group."

Bill Wassmuth was another member of the clergy, whom Broadbent had heard others label as a bleeding heart liberal. Wassmuth's church, St. Pius, was known around the area for taking up one cause or another; during the 60's it'd even been called a hot bed of anti-war radicals.

"The problem with that," David Cohen picked up, "is that the Jewish faith won't be represented, since we don't have a synagogue or a rabbi in town."

"I see," Rick Morse acknowledged, and nodded.

"Maybe we can work it out another way," Dina Tanners suggested, her eyes glittering with intensity. "Rick, why can't we make your group more broadly based than just the clergy? Maybe we can include prominent townspeople as well."

"You mean form some kind of human rights coalition?" Rick Morse asked.

"That's right," Tanners answered. "A group that can counteract Butler's racist material, and maybe offer citizens like Sid who have been harassed or otherwise victimized some degree of support."

"Might be hard to get people to join such a group," Morse cautioned, with a hint of sarcasm. "It was difficult enough to get certain members of the clergy to sign the statement we issued last year condemning the Aryans' racist propaganda. A few of my esteemed brethren refused to sign out of fear that their churches would be firebombed."

"Not to mention," David Cohen added, "that some of the more powerful businessmen in Coeur d'Alene would rather everyone forget about the Aryans so as not to draw negative attention to the town. The adverse publicity is hurting the tourism industry."

Rick Morse and Dina Tanners looked at one another across the table with expressions of knowing incredulity.

For his part Larry Broadbent kept wondering if these people were overreacting. A coalition to advance the cause of human rights, in his view, might further polarize the community along racial lines. As it was there were very few people of color in north Idaho, and only a handful of Jews. Probably the largest minority was the Coeur d'Alene Indian tribe. And most people in town would just as soon not get them stirred up.

"So where do we go from here?" Glen Walker asked, to break the silence.

Rosen shifted his eyes to Broadbent, then to Stalder. "You people live in Coeur d'Alene, five miles away," the restaurant owner explained. "I'm right down the road from those crazies. Hell, they could burn my place to the ground before you got out here."

"I can't say as I blame you for being afraid and angry, Sid," Marshall Mend sympathized, his normally playful, happy features turned sour. "If I knew this neo-Nazi business was going on I may have thought twice before moving my family up here from Los Angeles last summer."

"I don't understand you people," Dina Tanners countered, a storm warning in her dark eyes. "You can't let these thugs intimidate you."

"I have to look at Butler and his people every day," Rosen emphasized. "They come into town every morning, and hang out at the Owl Café, where Butler opens his mail. You should see how much money comes to that guy in the mail. Hundreds, maybe thousands of dollars a day. The money pours in from people all over the country who believe in Butler's cause, which is in itself scary.

"Just try to imagine how I feel when I'm in that café with Butler and his thugs, or I see them on the street, knowing they hate me, that they would like to exterminate—that's their word, exterminate—me.

"Plus, this stuff is hurting my business. People are afraid to come in."

"We'll do all we can to support and protect you," Dina Tanners finished.

Rosen slowly shook his head.

The group broke up with Sheriff Stalder promising that he would do everything in his power to track down whoever had spray-painted the slurs on Sid's restaurant, along with investigating the reports that someone had been following Rosen. Rick Morse and Dina Tanners also agreed to get together within the next week to talk further about forming some kind of coalition of citizens to combat racism in the community.

Larry Broadbent walked with Sheriff Merf Stalder out to the parking lot. They paused next to Broadbent's car.

"What do you think, Larry?" Stalder asked, leveling his gaze on the taller man.

"I don't know," Broadbent answered. He stuck his hand in his pocket, and began fingering the coins. This thing seemed far beyond him. "Way I figure, it's probably just an isolated incident, a prank, most likely a couple of lunkhead drunks out on the town. Or someone that might be angry at Rosen for some reason."

"You don't think it was an organized anti-Semitic group, like the Aryan Nations?"

"I don't know anything about Butler and his people, but I couldn't imagine they'd be so dumb as to stir up trouble in their own neighborhood."

"You're probably right," Stalder acknowledged. "But just for the hell of it why don't you check into this Aryan Nations bunch. Find out who they are, and what they're up to."

A smile played on Broadbent's lips. "You sure you know what you're doing, Merf? I'm not up much on civil rights issues, and business like that."

Stalder's eyes twinkled, and his face worked around into the warm, friendly grin that could charm the potatoes off a spud wagon.

"None of us know much about that stuff, Larry. So you get to be our expert on racism, bigotry, anti-Semitism and hate-related crimes."

"Thanks," Broadbent kidded. He reached for a cigarette. He had not had a smoke since before he walked into the restaurant—he was careful about polluting other people's air, especially since all that stuff came out about how a nonsmoker can get cancer from breathing someone else's smoke—and his entire body was calling out for nicotine.

"I'll do my best," he said, lighting up.

"I know you will," Stalder answered, before easing himself down into his car.

The Sheriff rolled down the window, and added, "You might begin with the Boise police. Seems to me I heard that Butler and his bunch got arrested down there last year on weapons charges. That might give you a leg up."

"Got it," Broadbent agreed.

Stalder started his car.

"By the way, Merf," Broadbent added. "I thought the reason we fought World War II was to get rid of the Nazis."

Stalder smiled. "So did I, Larry."

Broadbent leaned away from Stalder's car.

"See you back at the office," Stalder finished, and backed out of the driveway.

Larry Broadbent opened the door of his mud-splattered Buick, and sat heavily in the seat. He paused a moment before turning the ignition key. He was puzzled, and felt slightly intimidated by the assignment Stalder had handed him. But that did not make much difference to Broadbent. He was a good cop, one trained to follow orders. He would see what he could dig up about these Aryan Nations crackpots who allegedly paraded around their Hayden Lake compound in brown uniforms. He would try to learn if these neo-Nazis, as Rosen and the other Jews at the meeting he had just attended believed, were attempting to intimidate and harass people they did not believe deserved to live in the same society they did.

He started the engine of his car. He shifted into reverse, and was about to turn in the seat so he could check if there was anything behind him, when his eyes were drawn to the white lettering across the front of Sid Rosen's restaurant. For some reason he did not understand, the sight of the words Jewswine and KKK, along with the swastika, made him shudder inside. Maybe, just maybe, he thought, the people he had met with inside the restaurant were right; these slurs were more than a prank.

Nearly twenty years as a police officer had exposed him to a lot of hate and anger; he had investigated a slew of violent crimes—assaults, beatings, rapes, even murders—but this one hit him in a different way. He had never come up against anything like this before.

THREE

Marshall Mend walked around to the rear of his midnight-blue Cadillac, parked facing Librande's Lawnmower Repair Shop. The shop was located in the attached garage next to Librande's small wood house, on Government Way, near Sid Rosen's Restaurant. Mend unhooked the bungi cord that secured the partially open trunk. He lifted the trunk, and removed a rotary-style lawnmower. He placed the mower on the ground and pushed it through the front door of the shop.

A small bell jangled when he opened the door. He heard the growling sound of a power tool coming from the back room.

"Hello," Mend called. "Anyone here?"

The noise ceased abruptly, and a man's voice sounded, "Be right there."

Mend eyed the shop. Various-sized lawnmower head gaskets and other parts hung on nails along the wooden walls. In one corner on the floor was an old push lawnmower, its wooden handle smooth from use, from which hung a hand-lettered "For Sale" sign. Several new, high-tech power mowers were also spaced around the floor. Scraps of paper cluttered the wooden counter. No cash register in sight, Mend figured that Librande, like so many others in the area, operated out of his pocket.

Despite the previous month's incident at Sid Rosen's Restaurant, Marshall Mend liked living in Coeur d'Alene. His real estate career was coming together nicely; in less than six months he had earned more money than he had the entire previous year in Southern California as a sales representative for a meat company. Furthermore, money went further in north Idaho, where the cost of living was much less than it was in Los Angeles, where Mend grew up. Marshall was the only member of his family who made the break from Southern California; his parents still resided in the predominantly Jewish Wilshire District of Los Angeles, a neighborhood in which they felt safe and comfortable, surrounded by people of their own kind.

Mend, raised around mostly other Jews, never became afflicted with that sense of anxious apartness with which he had seen others of his faith suffer. Mend simply felt no sense of inferiority because of his religion. Beyond that, Marshall wore his Jewishness like a loose garment. He was, as he found out once he had moved to north Idaho, the equivalent of a Jack Mormon, a lapsed Latter Day Saints member. Further, he attended the Presbyterian Church, where his wife, Dolly, regularly worshipped.

Mend was happy to be out of crowded, polluted and crime-ridden Southern California. Some years back he and his wife had made the decision not to raise their daughter in Los Angeles, with all the drugs, behavioral problems, violence and other distractions into which children seemed to be drawn. Life in north Idaho was slower and safer; since moving here, the Mends had abandoned the siege-mentality tactics people in a big city automatically adopt. He and his wife had even taken to leaving the doors of their house unlocked. The one hundred twenty-one thousand dollars they had paid for the three thousand square foot house with the spectacular view of the lake was easily a seventh of what they would have paid in Los Angeles.

Mend, however, had lost some of his new-found innocence after Sid Rosen's Restaurant had been defaced with anti-Semitic slurs. Since then he and his family had reinstated their old LA habit of locking the doors of their house, whether home or not.

Mend's musings were interrupted when Sam Librande appeared from the back room of the shop. The dark-haired, flinty little man moved on his feet like a sprinter stepping to the blocks. Librande had shining dark eyes, and a small thin mouth over a dimpled, grizzled chin.

"What can I do for you?" Librande asked.

"This thing starts hard," Mend answered, aware Librande was giving him the once over. "It also needs sharpening."

"Fifteen bucks plus parts for the tune-up," Librande posed. "Another seven-fifty to sharpen her."

"Sounds fair." Mend responded in kind to Librande's habit of being spare with words.

Librande removed a tag from a drawer under the counter.

"Name?" he asked, clenching a yellow pencil in his grease-smudged fingers.

Mend told him.

"Phone number?"

Mend gave it to him.

"Be a week or so," Librande advised. He looked quickly toward the back room, then back at Mend. "I'm kinda jammed up right now.

"No problem."

Mend smiled at Librande. A born peddler, Marshall always felt most comfortable when he established a warm connection with someone. "I don't know what is hurting real estate sales more, all this rain causing the lawns to grow so fast you can't keep them cut, or the high interest rates."

"That what you do? Real estate?" Librande asked.

"Yep." Mend reached into his shirt pocket, retrieved a business card, and handed it to Librande. You never knew, the guy might need to buy or sell some property.

Librande took Mend's business card, and offered a quick, understanding smile. He tore off the end of the repair claim tag, and handed it to Mend. He tied the other half on the handle of Mend's lawnmower.

"You know why the interest rates are so high, don't you?" Librande queried, his eyes like dark, wet stones.

"I figured it was still a hangover from the Carter administration," Mend offered, his smile rearranging his features. A Republican, he had been incensed at the way Jimmy Carter had handled the economy.

"Ah," Librande responded, waving a hand at Mend like the real estate man should know better. "Carter was only the front for them kikes that run the Federal Reserve Board. The Federal Reserve and all the other Jewboys that control the money in this country."

Librande leaned his corded, hairy forearms on the counter. His eyes were afire, and his jaw muscles jumped. He moved his face to within a few inches of Mend's.

Shocked by Librande's anger, hatred and overt anti-Semitism,

Mend quickly wondered if Librande would say these things if he knew he was a Jew.

"We ought to go back on the gold standard, I tell you," Librande added. "Make our money worth something again."

The lawnmower repair man reached under the counter. Mend had a quick, stabbing fear Librande knew he was a Jew after all, and was going after a gun or some other kind of weapon.

"While we're at it," Librande continued, as he pawed around the shelf under the counter, "we should get rid of the IRS. Nothing more than a glorified collection agency for the Zionist Occupied Government."

"No doubt we all pay too much in taxes," Mend said. Though believing his statement, he was not particularly attached to the sentiment. He was attempting to humor Librande, rather than engage in this conversation. He wanted the hell out of there as fast as he could.

"Damned right we pay too much in taxes," Librande steamed. He withdrew a couple of pamphlets from the drawer under the counter and dropped them in front of Mend.

Mend felt a shiver run up his back as he recognized the red and blue crest on the front of the pamphlets. It was the Aryan Nations swastika.

"We pay all those taxes to support the lazy niggers and spics," Librande added, hate dripping from his voice. "All they do is fornicate and have more kids so they can collect more welfare, which you and I are paying for. The goddamned country is being ruined by those mongrels. North Idaho is one of the only places left in the U.S not lousy with niggers, spics, slopeheads, homos, and Jews."

Mend wanted to tell this guy he was full of it, and identify himself as a Jew just to see what Librande's reaction might be. But he did not. The reason he did not was all too clear to him; Mend was afraid to tell Librande the truth. He did not fear Librande personally; what gave him reason to pause was *who* Librande might tell about Mend being a Jew.

"Here's the way out of the mess this country's in," Librande added, pointing a finger at the pamphlets. "Take these along with you and read them."

Mend reached for the pamphlets. He decided it would be less trouble to pick them up and get out of there.

"These people know what they're talking about," Librande continued, watching Mend scoop up the pamphlets. "The Aryan Nations wants to protect the white race. They want to give us a place to live free of mongrels, homos and Jews."

Mend smiled a sickly smile, turned, and made for the door.

"Think about it," Librande called from behind him.

"Trust me, I will," Mend returned. Then he thought, you know what trust me means, don't you, Librande? It's LA for screw you.

Mend pulled the door open, and stepped outside the small shop. He climbed quickly into his car, and started it. He drove a few blocks before pulling to the curb in front of a small park. He was so angry and anxious he thought he might get sick to his stomach.

Mend's hand was shaking as he leafed through the pamphlets Librande had given him. It was all there, the hate, and the blaming of Jews, blacks and other minorities for the country's problems. Mixed-race marriages were considered an abomination, and whites who married non-whites were branded race traitors and were to be executed. Jews, bankers, gays, and all non-whites who consorted with whites were judged by the Aryans to be guilty of a capital crime and were to be exterminated. Further, the Aryans offered Biblical justification for their hate, racism, bigotry and anti-Semitism. Mend shook his head. The Klan reads from the Bible while lynching a black, he thought. Quite a book.

It was not necessarily the hate-language and bigotry in these pamphlets that bothered Mend. He had seen and heard all this rhetoric before and had previously read some of the Aryan Nations literature. Today's experience with Librande had been different. It was more than just reading something in a pamphlet. Mend had actually come face to face with a man who, because of his belief system, was convinced that the Jewish man was guilty of committing a capital crime punishable by death. Sam Librande wanted to exterminate him.

Mend was stunned that there were actually people in this community—Marshall Mend's community—who wanted to kill him. Such a reality was equally frightening and maddening. Mend had never before experienced this brand of anti-Semitism first-hand. It kicked up a fear deep within him, a feeling akin to what he imagined his ancestors felt in the face of the pogroms in Russia, or as they waited for the SS to come for them in Nazi-occupied countries of Europe. He was suddenly afraid of what the future might bring for him and his family. He even gave some thought to contacting the Undersheriff—what was his name—who attended the meeting the previous month at Sid Rosen's restaurant, and telling him about what had happened today. Mend quickly dismissed that idea. What were the authorities going to do? Arrest a nut-job hatemonger like Sam Librande for what he thought or believed, no matter how twisted and hateful?

Marshall Mend felt something else as he sat in the front seat of his car, staring at the venomous Aryan literature. That he had not had the guts to stand up to Librande and tell the lawnmower repairman that he was a Jew and proud of it, enraged Mend. Then he wondered why, if he was so proud of being a Jew, did he hide that fact from Sam Librande? Why had he, since moving to north Idaho, downplayed his Jewishness? Beyond the rage, Mend was ashamed. And shame was a hard emotion to swallow for such a proud and optimistic man.

Mend drove away from the curb, and, for the first time since he owned the Cadillac, found himself wishing he was not driving such a distinguishable car.

FOUR

"A Mr. Bob Hughes is here to see you," the female voice sounded through the telephone intercom.

Bob Hughes? Broadbent thought. I don't think I know any Bob Hughes.

Larry Broadbent glanced around his tiny, cluttered office, as if wondering where his visitor might sit.

"Send him in," Broadbent said into the intercom speaker.

Through his office door appeared a stocky, handsome man with a full head of graying hair, whom Broadbent pegged immediately as a federal government official. They all had a certain way of dressing— gray or blue suits, white shirt, wing-tipped shoes, rep tie—and moved with a purposeful nonchalance, like every one of them had learned their demeanor out of the same manual, which they had.

"Officer Broadbent? I'm Bob Hughes, with the Community Relations Service of the Department of Justice out of Seattle," he said, a slight trace of southern accent.

"Sit down," Broadbent offered, chuckling to himself as he shook Hughes' hand. "Coffee?"

Hughes took the chair on the other side of Broadbent's desk. The federal agent smiled politely, showing a space between his two upper front teeth. Hughes was well built, as if he spent a few days a week in the gym, an observation that prompted Broadbent to remind himself to get into an exercise routine one of these days.

"No coffee, thanks," Hughes responded. "I've had enough

already this morning."

Hughes dropped his business card on Broadbent's desk.

Broadbent picked up the card and ran his thumb over the embossed printing that read, **Bob Hughes, Mediator, Community Relations Service, U.S. Department of Justice**.

"What's a Mediator do?"

"I work within a community to attempt to resolve problems and strife before they escalate into criminal activity."

"Sounds like your job is to try to put guys like me out of one," Broadbent jabbed.

"Not really," Hughes answered with a smile. "I'm more like the smoke jumper of a fire fighting crew that attempts to put out hot spots before they develop into a firestorm."

Broadbent leaned back in his swivel-chair, laced his fingers behind his head, and looked across the desk. "So, what can I do for you?"

"You asked Justice for information on Richard Butler, along with background checks on some of the other people associated with the Aryan Nations."

"That's right," Broadbent responded. He watched Hughes pull a manila folder overflowing with papers out of his briefcase, and place it on the desk in front of him. The thickness of the folder startled the Undersheriff.

Broadbent considering asking if the Post Office was on holiday—otherwise Hughes could have mailed him this stuff—but thought better of it. As a rule these federal boys did not make unnecessary trips.

"Figured it'd be best if I came here in person to go through this with you," Hughes explained, as if reading Broadbent's mind. "It's kind of complicated."

Broadbent untangled his fingers, brought his hands around in front of him, and instinctively reached into his shirt pocket for his cigarettes.

"Care for one," he asked, holding the pack out in front of him.

"Don't use 'em."

"Mind if I do?"

"Not at all."

Broadbent reached behind him and cracked the window a couple of inches. Then lit up.

"Looks as though you're sitting right in the middle of a hornet's nest," Hughes began, opening the folder.

"You don't say," Broadbent answered. He had a sick feeling in his stomach that his theory about Butler and his cronies being a bunch of harmless kooks running around the forest was about to be taken apart.

"Let's begin with Butler," Hughes said. He worked the top two or three sheets of paper off the stack and moved them into the center of the desk.

Broadbent leaned forward to get a better look at the eight-by-ten glossy photo of Richard Butler, the type taken on the sly by an undercover cop. At first glance the Aryan Nations chief reminded Broadbent of someone's favorite uncle. Butler had pointed but not sharp features, weathered skin hanging off a square, chiseled chin, and a full head of steel gray hair—more white than gray at the temples—that he parted and combed to one side. However, it was Butler's eyes that drew Broadbent's attention. They were dark and cold, like stones in a stream bed, and partially obscured by fleshy, wrinkled lids. Eyes, Broadbent thought, that would cause him to pause while looking through a book of mug shots.

"Butler moved here in the early 1970's," Hughes began.

You came all the way here from Seattle to tell me that? Broadbent thought. We already *know* when he moved to north Idaho.

"Butler was an aircraft worker, a machinist, in California," Hughes continued in a monotone, as if he knew it all by heart. "He became a follower of John Wesley Swift, who founded the white supremacist Church of Jesus Christ Christian in the 1940's. When Swift died, Butler assumed control of the church. He changed the church's name to the Aryan Nations, and moved it lock, stock and barrel into your backyard."

"Great. Any idea why he chose this area?"

"Your guess is as good as mine. Justice feels as though he selected this area as his headquarters because of the low number of minorities residing here. He has a history of making statements about the need to establish a white homeland, and this is the place he wants to do it."

"He actually wants to establish a white homeland here? In north Idaho?" an incredulous Broadbent queried.

"He's been busy trying to do exactly that in the seven years he's been up here. Most of it behind the scenes."

"How do you mean?" Broadbent asked, his police officer interest piqued.

"The first thing you have to realize about Butler is that he's a smart cookie," Hughes explained, looking Broadbent dead in the eyes. "That's what sets him and the current leaders of the various white supremacist groups apart from those who have led the movement in the past. This crop of guys are bright, and they are masters at manipulating the media.

"You get someone who's bright, has good organizational skills and knows how to manipulate the media. Add the ingredient of hate… you have a very volatile situation," Hughes completed. "Especially if the economy takes a downturn."

Broadbent thought about that one. The economy around Coeur d'Alene had been tough the past few years, what with the national recession. Add the closing of the silver mines in Kellogg, the next town to the east, and you have thousands of area people thrown out of work. People who had never before received public assistance were queued up at the welfare office. In that sense, north Idaho was ripe for the Aryan Nations to move in and spread their hate message about how blacks and Mexicans were taking all the jobs, or that the "Jew-run U.S. Government" was enticing companies to close their operations and move to Mexico, Thailand and other places where non-whites worked for practically nothing.

"I don't know a lot about these hate groups," Broadbent admitted, a twinkle in his brown eyes, and a small smile playing at his lips. "But, I always heard that their leaders and members weren't too smart."

Hughes was busy rearranging the papers on the desk.

"You know the old story, what has four teeth, and an IQ of 70?"

Broadbent posed.

"Can't say as I do," Hughes answered, and looked up.

"The front row of a Klan rally."

A smile tugged at Hughes' lips, though his eyes did not seem too amused.

"You have to lose that perception if you're going to understand what is going on in Hayden Lake," Hughes admonished. "Butler has given the white supremacist movement what they've been lacking: a leader who can unify the Klan, National Alliance, Posse Comitatus, White Aryan Resistance and other hate groups."

Broadbent looked blankly at Hughes. Of the groups the federal agent mentioned, only the Klan rang a bell with him. Most of the information Broadbent knew about the Klan he learned from watching a television program entitled "Bad Moon Rising."

"Butler has brought all these groups under the Aryan Nations leadership—his leadership—and has been recruiting high-profile white supremacists into his hierarchy," Hughes continued. "These groups and individuals all have one thing in common: they hate Jews, blacks, Hispanics, Asians, homosexuals, bankers, the IRS, and anyone who they deem is polluting or ruining the white race."

"What do they expect to do?" Broadbent asked. "Force all the people they don't like to move out of America?"

Hughes withdrew a paperback book out of his briefcase. The title, *The Turner Diaries*, was embossed in gold across the black and red cover.

"This book is the white supremacists' blueprint for action—their bible," he said, pushing the paperback across the desk to Broadbent.

"It details the preparations for the coming race war. So far, Butler has set the stage for the plan of revolution outlined in this book, almost to the punctuation marks... I'd suggest you read it."

"I will," Broadbent said, taking the book from Hughes. All of this seemed unbelievable to him. On the other hand, what Hughes was revealing served to give credence to the warnings of Dina Tanners, Rick Morse, and the others wishing to form a Task Force on Human Relations.

"Who are these other people, the White Aryan Resistance, Posse Comitatus, and National Alliance?" Broadbent asked, while studying the cover of the book. He decided to stick his ego into his desk drawer, and learn what he could from Hughes.

"The White Aryan Resistance is primarily an information clearing house, though they have members scattered throughout the United States," Hughes explained. "It was started by Tom Metzger, a former John Bircher and Klan member who ran for Congress in California. Metzger won the primary but got swamped in the general election.

"The Posse Comitatus is one of the many tax protest groups located throughout the United States. They—along with almost every other white supremacist group—believe that Jews control the government, including the IRS. Posse Comitatus is headed by Gordon Kahl, and they're an extremely violent group.

"The National Alliance is a loose-knit group of fascist organizations that follow the ideas of William Pierce," Hughes concluded.

The federal agent slid another piece of paper out of the folder, and positioned it in the middle of the desk. It was an organizational chart. The top-most box contained Richard Butler's name.

"This chart shows Butler's genius," Hughes explained, while tapping a rhythm on the paper with the clicker end of his ball-point pen. "By stitching the various white supremacist groups together he now has essentially 20,000 white supremacists under his influence. Maybe under his control would be a more appropriate term," the federal agent added.

"In addition he has over 200,000 sympathizers, people around the country who offer financial and political support to the white supremacist cause."

Broadbent gulped. "Do any of these avowed white supremacists people live around here?"

Once again Hughes leveled his gaze on Broadbent, and said, "More every week."

"What does that mean?"

Hughes withdrew a copy of the Aryan Nations newsletter from the manila folder. He placed it on the desk in front of Broadbent, who glanced quickly through the four-page, crudely produced publication. What Broadbent read caused him to nervously reach for another cigarette. The newsletter was dedicated almost entirely to enticing white supremacists to move to north Idaho, which according to Richard Butler had been selected as the headquarters of the future white homeland.

"Are you trying to tell me that these kind of people are actually moving here?" an incredulous Broadbent asked.

"We're estimating that in the last couple of years three to four hundred white supremacists have moved into the area from other parts of the country. That is in addition to the several dozen or so living on the compound."

Larry Broadbent flushed with embarrassment. This thing was beginning to mess with his professional pride. About the only thing he had been able to come up with since Sheriff Merf Stalder asked him to look into the Aryan Nations was that Richard Butler, along with a couple of his confederates, were arrested the previous spring in Boise for carrying concealed weapons in a public place. Butler and his neo-Nazi associates were in Boise to conduct a public meeting to recruit new members into the Aryan Nations movement, but the hotel owner, upon finding out who they were and what they were up to, canceled the gathering. The hotel owner asked the police to be on hand in case there would be any trouble, and the Boise police found guns on Butler and the others during a routine check. Broadbent had not placed much stock in that incident. This was Idaho, he had reasoned, and many people carried guns.

Hughes placed another 8x10 black and white glossy in front of Broadbent. It was a picture of a clean-cut, handsome man obviously caught unsuspecting by the camera as he walked out of a retail store.

"This is one of the people who has moved into the Hayden Lake Aryan Nations compound," Hughes explained. "His name is Louis Beam, former head of the Texas branch of the Klan. Beam has been implicated in the firebombing of Vietnamese fishing boats in Galveston Bay."

Broadbent remembered hearing about the bombings. They occurred over a several month period, the victims impoverished

Vietnamese fishermen. As he recalled there were injuries.

"Beam has been appointed by Butler as ambassador-at-large of the Aryan Nations," Hughes explained, further. "Which on its own means nothing. What *is* significant is that Beam is a computer whiz. We have it on good source that he is in the process of creating a computer network that will electronically link the Aryan Nations with white supremacist groups throughout the United States and Canada. Instant communications. A hot line for hate groups."

"What does that do for them?" Broadbent asked.

"It gives them the opportunity to relay information between groups in an instantaneous, untraceable way. It transforms what was once a bunch of splinter groups into one cohesive, ideologically monolithic force. One dedicated to achieving its means, by armed force if necessary."

For the first time since assigned this case, Larry Broadbent was beginning to comprehend the implications of what was happening in north Idaho. There was much about the Aryans he did not understand, their theology for instance, and why they had chosen Hayden Lake as their headquarters. But Broadbent was beginning to understand the kind of menace several hundred armed zealots might pose, not only to north Idaho, but to the entire northwest. Deep within him a tiny alarm about what was occurring at Hayden Lake sounded, the alarm Broadbent had learned in his years in law enforcement to trust.

Once again Broadbent lowered his eyes to the organization chart. Louis Beam's name occupied one of the several boxes that made up the second row, located directly under Richard Butler's name.

Following each of the other names in the second row of boxes was the name of the organization they headed or belonged to. These names did not mean much to Broadbent, names like Robert Miles, William Potter Gale, David Duke, John Ross Taylor and others, names the Undersheriff strongly suspected he had come to know well over the next several months.

"Does anyone actually believe their hate propaganda?" Broadbent asked.

"Afraid so," Hughes answered, thoughtfully. "Butler and his group appeal mostly to alienated whites, people who are struggling to stay above the poverty line, or those who because of the shifts in the economy or other circumstances have sunk below it. Butler also recruits heavily in prisons by exploiting racial tensions inherent in those places."

Broadbent understood how white inmates were susceptible to white supremacist ideology. They were in the minority in most correctional facilities, which were run as much by the ethnic gangs within them as by the warden and guards. Most whites locked up in penitentiaries tended to be poor and undereducated. Wealthy, educated white-collar criminals, Broadbent considered—with the brand of emotional detachment and non-judgment he had picked up from his years in police work—wound up on probation or spent a few months at a minimum security 'country-club' correctional facility.

"The white supremacist movement," Hughes explained further, "is basically broken down into two distinct factions: Christian Patriot, and Christian Identity. Both groups have a common belief system, which is based on the supposition that the United States is fundamentally and by constitutional mandate strictly a white Christian country. The Christian Patriots, those belonging to groups like Posse Comitatus, Golden Mean Society and the Klan see it as their duty to save the country from the IRS, Federal Reserve System, and the federal government itself, all of which they feel are run by Jews, or operate heavily under Jewish influence.

"The Christian Identity faction believes the same things as the Christian Patriots, but they take the basis for their ideology from the Bible, instead of the Constitution."

Broadbent noticed his watch. He could not believe they had been at this over an hour. He was getting a cram course about an entire underground hate group network he had not even known existed before Hughes showed up at his office. "These people actually use the Bible to justify exterminating Jews and people of color?"

"That's right," Hughes clarified. He looked ruefully at Broadbent. "What did Mark Twain say about people who love their neighbor as long as that neighbor believes in the same things they do? Otherwise they cut their neighbor's throat."

The Department of Justice official withdrew a couple of pamphlets from his briefcase, and slid them across the desk to Broadbent. One was entitled, "Your Heritage"; the other, "The Two Seeds Of Genesis." Both exhibited the Aryan Nations swastika prominently on the front cover.

"You much of a scholar of the Bible?" Hughes asked.

"Not really. Like about everyone else I studied it as a kid, and every once in awhile I go to church."

"Look through these pamphlets when you get a chance. They'll show you how these white supremacists have come up with the notion that Christ was an Aryan, and that whites are the chosen race and are mentally and spiritually superior to people of color."

"Christ an Aryan? Like Hitler?" an astonished Broadbent asked, chuckling despite himself. "That's a new one on me."

"Was for me, too," Hughes answered, with a smile of his own.

The two men sat silently for a few moments, the only sound the low hiss of warm air flowing through the waffle-shaped ceiling convector.

"Maybe your people should take a ride out there sometime?" Hughes said, a twinkle in his eye. "That is if you can come up with an official reason to visit the Aryan compound."

"Let me see…" Broadbent pulled open the right-hand drawer of his desk. He sent his fingertips dancing across the tops of file folders until he found the one he was looking for. He withdrew the manila folder from the drawer, opened it, and read quickly through its contents.

"A few months ago," he began, while reading, "the county building inspector went through the Aryan Nations compound, and discovered a number of code violations. Minor infractions such as not enough exit doors, and what exit doors that exist are not properly marked. So far Butler has refused to comply with the county's order to repair the safety violations. It would be within my domain to go out there and look around."

"Might be worth your while," Hughes said, and stood. He gathered his material and notes together, and slid them into his briefcase. He snapped the briefcase shut, and turned for the door.

"Good luck. Call if you need me."

"Will do."

FIVE

On his way to Hayden Lake, Larry Broadbent recalled mentioning to Bob Hughes that the Aryans had not broken any laws that he knew of. He thought the feds and local authorities were spending taxpayer money investigating a group that, though their views were loathsome, appeared to be comprised of law-abiding citizens.

Hughes had calmly looked Broadbent in the eye, and replied, "Our experience is that groups that openly advocate violence will eventually commit it."

That had brought up the cop fear in Broadbent. It would not be long before word got back to the Aryan Nations—if it had not already—that Broadbent was the Kootenai County police officer in charge of investigating them.

Broadbent steered his car along Rimrock Road, through high meadow pasture, until he came to a white sign at the end of a dirt road intersecting the county highway. On the sign was a large edition of the Aryan Nations swastika, under which were the words: **Church of Jesus Christ Christian, Aryan Nations. Services Sunday at 11, Wednesday at 7**. The winding dirt road, barely wide enough for one car, disappeared into a stand of pine and fir trees at the crest of the hill.

"Into the camp of the enemy," Broadbent muttered to himself.

Steering his car off the asphalt road, Broadbent got that tight, tingling sensation in his lower throat, the feeling he always got just before he approached some potentially dangerous situation. It stayed with him as he drove carefully along the dirt road, his car kicking up a plume of dust. He entered the thick cluster of trees, and came upon a guard shack on the left. A thick iron pipe gate prevented him from driving any farther. The black on white sign hanging on the guard shack warned, **WHITES ONLY**.

A man in camouflage clothing, and packing twin .357 Magnums on his belt, appeared out of the guard shack.

"What can I do for you?" the guard asked, staring down with ice-blue eyes. He was tall, with well-tended, bunchy muscles of a powerlifter, and dark hair and matching thick beard. He wore a black beret with a silver cross on the front. On each shoulder was the red and blue Aryan swastika.

Broadbent reached slowly into the vest pocket of his jacket for his wallet. He opened it, and flashed his badge.

"Undersheriff Larry Broadbent. I'm here to check if the building code safety violations have been repaired."

The guard's attitude shifted from suspicion to disdain. The Aryans, Broadbent had learned, viewed law enforcement officers as carrying out the mandates of the "illegal Zionist Occupied Government." They felt no compulsion to obey the laws of the U.S. government; they had their own laws.

"Hold on a minute," the guard said, without humor or friendliness. He stepped back into the shack, and closed the door behind him.

Broadbent watched the man say a few words into the phone. The guard nodded, hung up, and emerged from the shack.

"You can go on up," he instructed, less stiffly. "The office will be the fourth building on your left. Reverend Butler will see you."

The guard turned and pushed down the lever that actuated the barrier. The pipe gate scissored up, and Broadbent drove through.

The car crested the hill. Off to the left on a flat, treeless area several men in camouflage gear were going through military maneuvers. To one side was a tall, reed-thin man in a neatly pressed, starched camouflage outfit, black beret, reflector sunglasses, and holstered sidearm. He smacked a riding crop into the palm of his hand to the rhythm of the cadence he was calling. The men high-stepped double-time, rifles held across the chest, through a course of rubber tires lying flat on the grass.

Broadbent remembered Hughes telling him that a surprising number of white supremacists were former military men. There were even some former high-ranking officers of the U.S. military in the Aryan hierarchy who took up the cause upon retiring from the service.

Broadbent was shocked and embarrassed that he had not been up here before to find out what was going on.

He eased his car to a stop in front of the building marked "Office." To his right was a guard tower, from which a uniformed man with an automatic weapon cradled in his arms watched him.

In front of the office building, standing stiffly in his heavily-starched khaki uniform was a man Broadbent recognized immediately as Richard Butler. The dark, stern, probing eyes that had caught Broadbent's attention in Hughes' photograph watched him as he approached.

"Here I go," Broadbent said. He drew a deep breath, opened the car door and stepped out.

"Reverend Butler," he said, courteously, "I'm Larry Broadbent of the Kootenai County Sheriff's Office."

"So I'm told," Butler answered, with a hint of humor. He had a husky, smoker's voice.

"I know of your work," Butler finished, more seriously.

Broadbent's right eyebrow arched. "I wanted to stop by to check that the items red-tagged by the building inspector have been taken care of."

"Of course you do," Butler countered. "Take a look around. We have nothing to hide."

"Thanks."

"If it mattered," Butler added, almost playfully, "I could save you the time by telling you that I haven't gotten around to repairing the items on the list of violations the building inspector sent out."

"I'll look around," Broadbent finished.

"Might as well start here," Butler said, extending his arm in the direction of the office.

Broadbent entered the small, wood building. He walked into a reception area, in which a pleasant-looking woman in her forties sat behind a metal desk.

"This is my secretary, Betty Tate," Butler introduced.

Broadbent smiled and nodded.

He looked over the woman's head into a small, cluttered office that Broadbent assumed belonged to Butler. To the Undersheriff's left, down a short hallway, was a print shop. Four men looking to be in their twenties and early thirties were busy running various machines, including an offset printing press. Two of the men wore pale-blue shirts complete with the Aryan swastika on each shoulder.

"We fill about two thousand requests a week for literature about the Aryan Nations," Butler boasted, from behind Broadbent. "That doesn't include the hundreds of orders we get every week for cassette recordings of my sermons."

Broadbent nodded nonchalantly, though startled by the man's claim. If Butler could be believed this print shop filled over a hundred thousand requests each year for material that advocated white supremacy and the extermination of entire groups of people. Unbelievable, Broadbent thought.

Broadbent walked to the rear of the print shop. What he saw confirmed Butler's earlier statement: despite being ordered by the county building inspector to do so, the Aryans had not installed an exit sign over the rear door.

Before he had the chance to push out the back door, Broadbent noticed the map of the United States mounted on the plywood wall. Colored in tan were Washington, Oregon, Idaho, Wyoming and Montana. Underneath, in bold letters were the words: THE ARYAN NATION: A TERRITORIAL IMPERATIVE.

Broadbent walked outside, where he continued the charade of pretending to be checking if Butler had complied with the order to repair various building code violations. There were thirteen buildings spread around the property; the twenty acre compound was a small, self-contained village. In addition to a wood church and a school, there were several large mobile homes, residences for an undetermined number of families, along with a cluster of log cabins. Farther out there were over a dozen camper trailers spotted around the property. Broadbent did a quick estimate, and figured there were probably 75-100 people living at the Aryan Nations compound, of which about two dozen were currently engaged in the paramilitary training exercises on the nearby drill field.

Broadbent walked towards the church, adjacent to the one-room school. He glanced into the school and saw about twenty kids being taught by a male instructor dressed in a pale-blue shirt with the red and blue Aryan swastika sewn on each shoulder. He stepped inside the knotty pine church. A woman was sweeping the polished concrete floor.

"Can I help you?" the middle-aged woman asked, pleasantly. She wore her honey-colored hair in a bun on the back of her head, and had widely spaced, inquisitive blue eyes, lined heavily off the corners. Her red and black flannel shirt and jeans fit her trim form snugly.

"Just having a peek," Broadbent answered. He glanced around the plain church. A small, varnished wooden lectern stood at the front; and built into the front wall behind the lectern was a large stained glass window featuring the Aryan Nations swastika. A hundred and fifty or so folding chairs stood in rows like birds waiting to be fed.

"You live on the compound?" he asked.

"Yep."

"How long?" Broadbent continued. As an afterthought, he added, "I'm not disturbing you, am I?"

"Gosh, no," she said, and laughed a good, free and open laugh, the kind Broadbent heard on the farm from women as yet uncomplicated by life's big issues. "I'll take any excuse I can get to give this broom a rest."

The woman placed her broom against a nearby wall, and stepped back to where Broadbent was waiting.

"We've been here a little over two years. We moved to north Idaho after my husband and I lost our farm in Iowa. We'd been receiving Reverend Butler's newsletter for a few years, and decided to take him up on his invitation to live here."

"Your husband farm around here?" Broadbent asked. He wondered if the woman figured he was a prospective member of the movement, she was so friendly.

"He works in a machine shop in town. Our kids go to school on the compound."

"Sounds as though you like it here."

"We do," she answered, tossing Broadbent a knowing look. "Easier than fighting bankers and the government. Fewer problems here, raising kids and all. No drugs or coloreds, or things like that."

"I see." He found himself liking this woman. He even agreed with some of what she said, and was not certain if he should feel guilty about it.

"Just can't figure it," the woman went on.

"What's that?"

"Why the government would hand out all that money to those foreign countries, many of which are Communist, and won't even take care of its own people. Then they give amnesty to all those illegal aliens from Mexico and Central America, when most of them go on welfare as soon as they get to this country. Doesn't make sense," she added, a hardness creeping into her voice.

Larry Broadbent felt like a man standing on a dock watching someone he thought he knew drift away on a boat. The more this woman talked the less he identified with her.

"Best move along," Broadbent said. "Nice visiting with you."

"You, too," she finished, turning back for her broom.

Broadbent had seen all he needed to see. He walked across the gravel parking lot, and let himself into his car. He had driven past the guard station when he remembered something else Hughes told him about the Aryans: they were a very sexist organization. The men earned the money and were the warriors; their wives kept house, cooked and bore children. The women were kept away from commerce and military action.

Broadbent shook his head. This sure as hell wasn't the kind of police work he was used to. Being involved with this Aryan Nations investigation, along with participating in the formation of the Task Force, was cramming some very strange notions into his head. He was not even sure he wanted to learn half of what he was learning. Of one thing, however, he was certain: this Aryan Nations thing was much bigger and more ominous than he first believed. With white supremacists moving into north Idaho from all over the country to join Butler and the others already living here, and with the Aryan Nations' emphasis on military training, the area around Coeur d'Alene was being transformed into an armed camp. According to Broadbent's estimate, at the rate white supremacists were migrating here, sometime in the not too distant future Butler and his army would be strong enough that it'd damn near take a military operation to confront them. A frightening thought.

The Aryan Nations, Larry Broadbent now believed, was a group that needed close monitoring.

SIX

Hayden Lake

Richard Butler was pleased as he greeted the last of those filing out of his chapel after the regularly scheduled Wednesday evening church service. Tonight over 100 worshippers had packed the Aryan Nations chapel. Butler was exhilarated that his congregation was growing so rapidly. His message of creating a white homeland was falling on sympathetic ears; he was reaping an abundant harvest.

After saying goodbye to the last of his congregation, Richard Butler spun smartly on the heels of his spit-polished black shoes, and walked stiffly and briskly across the floodlit lawn, to the frame building that housed his office. He pulled open the door, and stepped into the reception area. His secretary, Betty Tate, was finishing up some last minute work. Later, she would head over to the chapel to perform her assigned task of straightening up and turning off the lights.

Butler smiled upon seeing her working this late. He could count on Betty; she had the absolute dedication Butler demanded from his followers. Further, the Tate woman belonged to a perfect Aryan family; her husband and son also believed completely and absolutely in the ideal of white supremacy and in the notion that the United States was created as a white Christian country.

"I loved your sermon," Betty Tate said, as she gathered papers off her desk in preparation to leave the office. "Very inspiring."

"Thank you," Butler answered.

"Goodnight, Reverend Butler."

"Goodnight, Betty."

He was grateful for Betty Tate's sensitivity to his schedule. Her hasty departure from the office was prompted less by her need to button up the chapel for the night than by her knowledge that Butler was about to meet with his top lieutenants.

Butler watched as she pulled the door closed behind her, and disappeared into the floodlit night. He stepped into his office, a moderately sized room whose butternut-colored paneled walls were cluttered with photos, shelves bending under the weight of books and stacks of papers, and miscellaneous certificates and mementos, including citations from the U.S. Government commending him for time spent in India as a civilian adviser during World War II. It was during Richard Girnt Butler's tour in India that he first began considering the concept of race consciousness. Seeing the teeming, starving hordes of Indians—mud people he later took to calling them—most living like swine, reproducing like wildfire, their only advancement towards civilization the result of British rule, had caused Butler to wonder about the future of the white race. Returning to the States after World War II, witnessing the growing menace of black and brown ghettos in the American cities, and rightly predicting the eventual flood of Hispanics and Asians into the U.S., Butler became alarmed. He became convinced that the only hope for the white race was for it to separate itself from other races, the mud people that would eventually and by sheer numbers pollute by intermarriage and therefore destroy the Aryan race. Butler believed such a condition would be an abomination, contrary to the will of God. The white race was destined to rule the other races—according to Butler corroborated by the Old Testament—proven by the reality that almost every advancement in civilization had been created by Aryans. If something was not done to stem the tide, those Aryans wise enough to avoid miscegenation would be ruled by colored people, an unacceptable, highly repulsive proposition for Richard Butler.

These were only perceptions and theories for Butler, until he discovered John Wesley Swift, founder of the Church of Jesus Christ Christian. Swift preached about the very things Butler felt. Further, he offered a solution: separation of the white race from the mud people and the abominable Jews, a plan to protect Aryan people from genetic contamination and eventual extinction. Swift advocated the creation of an all-white homeland, one in which laws against intermixing with colored people or fraternizing with Jews would be strictly enforced. The penalty for mud people or Jews that became sexually involved with whites was execution on the spot. The same penalty was to be meted out for any colored or Jew who even ventured into the all-white homeland. Drastic measures, maybe, but it was the only way to assure the purity and survival of the Aryan race.

Richard Butler ran his palm down the front of his pale blue shirt, a meaningless gesture of habit since his starched shirt still retained its crease. He paused for a moment, and studied the pair of photos hanging on the wall in back of his desk. One was Adolph Hitler, in Butler's view the greatest social visionary of all time; the other a grainy picture of Butler and John Wesley Swift. Butler was a young man then—thinner, his jet-black hair matching his intense dark eyes—and was standing next to the tall, reed-thin Swift, the latter's great mane of white hair distorted by the wind. The photo was taken a few months before Swift died and about a year after Butler's ordination as a minister in Swift's church. After Swift's death the leadership of the Church of Jesus Christ Christian had fallen to Richard Butler. One of Butler's first acts was to move the church from Southern California to Hayden Lake. North Idaho, with its minuscule non-white population, was a perfect home for the newly renamed Aryan Nations Church. And, in Butler's estimation, most of the white majority tacitly agreed with or at least accepted the Aryan ideology.

A noise in the outer office caused Butler to turn away from the framed photos. A man dressed in camouflage fatigues and spit-polished black boots entered the office.

"Eighty-eight," Keith Gilbert greeted, with a smile, before extending his right arm. H was the eighth letter of the alphabet, and double eights signified the greeting, 'Heil Hitler.'

"Heil Hitler," Butler answered, and returned the salute.

"Where're the others?" Gilbert asked, with his customary impatience.

"They're due," Butler answered, instinctively checking his watch. "Make yourself comfortable."

The dark-eyed intense-looking Gilbert sat in one of the folding chairs arranged in a circle at the far end of Butler's office. He stretched his legs out in front of him, crossed one polished black boot over the other, and took to fooling with his thick mustache.

Though the two men marched in ideological lock-step, there was much that set Butler and Gilbert apart. Richard Butler saw Keith Gilbert as a loose cannon, an unpredictable and violent renegade. Not that Butler had anything against employing violence when it was indicated, but Gilbert was undisciplined about it. He was a hothead, a hand grenade with the pin pulled.

The trouble between the two men had culminated in Gilbert leaving the Aryan Nations organization and forming his own group, the Social Nationalist Aryan Peoples Party. Butler had no idea how many members if any Gilbert had been able to recruit into his party. Not that it mattered. Gilbert was still active in the Aryan Nations and wanted the same things Richard Butler did, which was all the Minister cared about. Butler had been enough of a student of the Third Reich to understand that revolutionary race-purifying movements attracted any number of loyal though mentally unstable people. Individuals, Richard Butler knew, who made excellent soldiers of the revolution, only to be weeded out later. For now Butler would take all the warriors he could get, regardless of their mental stability.

"Hello, Bob," Butler said to the medium-sized, compact man who had just stepped into his office.

The baby-faced man had soft green eyes that upon closer inspection burned with intensity. It was Bob Mathews, the charismatic architect of the newly formed stormtrooper faction of the Aryan Nations, the Order. The Order had been modeled after the violent group of the same name in *The Turner Diaries*.

"Reverend Butler," Bob Mathews greeted, then turned towards

the other man. "Keith."

"How are you, Bob?" Gilbert answered.

Butler noted a slight change in Keith Gilbert's expression—his eyes softened and the insolence left his face—as he stood to shake Bob Mathews' hand. Gilbert both respected and feared the leader of The Order. And Mathews, hailing from nearby Metaline Falls, Washington, was a man to be feared. Unlike the brash, bombastic Keith Gilbert, Mathews had a quiet, cold explosiveness about him that sent a shiver up the spine of even the most hardened Aryan warrior. Of all the men in the white supremacist movement, Mathews was the one Richard Butler was most grateful to have on his side; he would put his hand into the fire for Bob Mathews.

Next, Sam Librande entered the room. The short, sinewy man warmly greeted Butler, Gilbert and Mathews, then took one of the chairs. The lawnmower repair shop owner lit a cigarette, and waited quietly for the others to arrive.

In moments the room was full of mostly young men in their twenties and thirties. Some wore traditional Aryan camouflage garb, others jeans and open-collared shirts. They were working-class men whose faces had been prematurely aged by hard times, loss of innocence, and countless days at soul-killing jobs.

Included in the group was Randy Duey, the husky, balding postal worker with thick, rimless glasses and furtive eyes; David Lane, tall and lean, dark hair combed neatly to one side, thick mustache, and handsome in a brooding sort of way; short, stocky, clean-shaven Walter West; blond-haired, blue-eyed William Soderquist, the highly intelligent John Birch Society and National Alliance member from

Salinas, California; and Denver Parmenter, the tall, bearded, lumbering son of an Air Force officer. Parmenter's face was flushed, the result of a strong affinity for booze.

"Shall we get started?" Butler posed.

The dozen white men formed a circle, and, in unison, solemnly recited: "I, as a free Aryan man, hereby swear an unrelenting oath upon the green graves of our sires, upon the children in the wombs of our wives, upon the throne of God almighty, to join together in a holy union with the brothers in this circle. From this moment I have the sacred duty to do whatever is necessary to deliver our people from the Jew and bring total victory to the Aryan race."

The men sat down.

"I called this meeting tonight," Butler began, "because we need to discuss some shifts in strategy."

Bob Mathews leaned his heavily-muscled forearms on his thighs, and thrust his head forward like a linebacker readying to enter the game for a goal line stand.

"How are things on your end, Bob?" Butler asked.

"We're a few months from being ready," Mathews answered, in his quiet, direct way. "Our recruitment of new members is taking longer than we figured. Everybody who comes in needs to be checked out. The ZOG-secret-police FBI is trying to infiltrate us."

Butler nodded. He completely trusted Mathews' judgment.

"It's also going to take us a little while longer to work out the details of our capitalization program," Mathews added, a wry smile playing at his lips.

Butler returned the smile. The Order's 'capitalization program' meant pulling together the equipment and technical expertise to begin counterfeiting money, along with a series of robberies, to buy weapons and provide a network of underground safe houses around the country in which Order members could hide. All, Butler thought happily, for the sole purpose of financing and equipping an underground army whose goal was to secure a white homeland in north Idaho; from there eventually to overthrow the "Jew-run government" of the United States.

Keith Gilbert raked his fingers through his thick hair. "I say we step things up a little. While we're sitting around talking, designing computer programs and burning crosses, niggers, kikes and beaners are moving into this area."

"Now we're talkin," Sam Librande agreed.

A few of the other men in the room nodded their approval.

"We ought to start putting the heat on the mud people and Jewboys," Gilbert added, "so they start moving out of the area, instead of the other way around."

"This has to be done right, Keith," Butler warned. "So far we've been successful in not bringing the local authorities down on us."

Keith Gilbert waved a hand. "What are we afraid of? The most that's gonna happen is that they'll conduct some farce of an investigation, like they did when we decorated the outside of Rosen's Restaurant…"

"Didn't we scare that hooked-nose kike?" Sam Librande interjected, his taut skin creased by a smile.

"Only good Jew is a dead Jew," West declared.

The men in Butler's office laughed openly.

"Besides," Gilbert picked up, "we all know that a lot of the boys with the badges are on our side. They might not want to come right out and say it but they are. The cops after all are the ones who have to deal with the crime-infested cities. They know what's happening to this country."

Butler took a deep breath. It came to him. It was perfect. Why not let Keith Gilbert stir up a little trouble, maybe scare some of the mud people and Jews into moving back to Los Angeles or San Francisco? It could work well; after all, Gilbert wasn't an official member of the Aryan Nations. He had been quite vocal to the press and to whomever would listen that he had started his own white supremacist movement, and had split from Richard Butler's group because they were more talk than action. Maybe, Butler mused, Gilbert could advance the Aryan Nations' ideals without exposing Butler and his followers to risk.

"You're free to do whatever you have to do, Keith," Butler finished, and watched the light come on in Gilbert's eyes. "As for us, we'll stick with our original plan of waiting for Bob to get things together before we move."

Gilbert smiled broadly. Richard Butler thought he looked like a teenager whose father had just given him permission to take the family car on a date for the first time.

SEVEN

Metaline Falls, Washington

Two dozen men in white robes, hoods pulled down low over their faces, encircled the twelve foot cross. The cross stood like a dark ragged scar against the night of a crescent moon and hard, glittering stars. In the background was the barn-shaped barracks building where Robert Mathews lived with several other members of The Order. Surrounding the dwelling were thick woods in which Mathews and the others had been executing secret paramilitary maneuvers over the past few months.

Mathews stepped forward. Eyes peering intensely like glowing chips of damp coal from the void inside his hood, Mathews slowly raised his right arm.

"The ZOG government has continually shown that it favors mud people over the holy and noble white race that built this great country."

Each of the men encircling the cross followed suit, and extended his right arm.

"It is time to invoke Yahweh on the kikes, mud people and white race traitors," Mathews continued, a chilling edge to his voice. "It is time to reclaim the land that is ours."

The group of silent men, right arms rigidly extended in front of them, stared with unseen eyes at the dark cross.

"Is the Order ready to capitalize itself?" Mathews asked.

"We are ready," a short man to his left responded.

"Is The Order prepared to invoke Yahweh on the kikes and mud people?" Mathews questioned, this time louder, with more feeling.

"We are now prepared to invoke Yahweh on the kikes and mud people," the entire group responded.

"Are you purified?" Mathews asked, his words reaching a crescendo.

"We will be purified before Yahweh begins," the men answered.

Mathews smiled an unseen smile. The identity of the government informer who had infiltrated the inner circle of the Aryan Nations was known.

"Then purify and invoke holy Yahweh on the tainted ones, on the descendants of Cain. May the ground run red with the blood of kikes, mud people, and race traitors."

Mathews reached into the opening at the side of his robe and fished his silver lighter out of his pants pocket. He flipped open the lid of the lighter with his thumb and spun the wheel to ignite it. The man closest to him handed him a stick with a gasoline-soaked swab of cloth at one end. Mathews held the lighter to the cloth, which came to flame with a burst.

"Yahweh on the descendants of Cain," he called, and held the flaming stick up to the cross. The cross instantly became an inferno.

"Yahweh! Yahweh!" the group chanted. Their right arms extended, faces golden, they stared at the furiously burning cross.

As the fire fell off some, Robert Mathews stepped into the middle of the circle. He unhitched the front of his robe, peeled back the cloth, and exposed the assault rifle slung over his shoulder. He held the rifle over his head with both hands. With a smile on his face, he turned slowly, taking turns looking directly at each of his fellow warriors. Each man he engaged with his eyes in turn unbuttoned his robe and exhibited an automatic weapon. By the time Mathews completed the circle the men surrounding him were holding their weapons over their heads. A communal chant like growling, distant thunder rose from the group.

"Yahweh to the kikes, mud people and race traitors," they chanted. "We pledge ourselves to reclaiming this white Christian homeland for its rightful owners."

Robert Mathews got the tight sensation in his throat he always experienced whenever he was about to embark on an exciting and dangerous mission. It was the feeling he got as a boy fixing in his sights a deer he had been tracking in the woods.

* * *

The Ahavath Synagogue on 17th and Bannock in Boise looked more like a small business than the home of one of the oldest Jewish congregations west of the Mississippi. The only hint of the true function of the gray stucco, one-story rectangular building was the small Star of David located over the front door. The building was quiet and the parking lot deserted this evening, though beginning the following day it would be the site of a week-long commemoration of the victims of the Holocaust, part of a ceremony performed in conjunction with synagogues across the United States.

A well-used white Chevy van turned off Bannock Street, one of

Boise's main streets, and drove slowly around to the rear of the temple. The van came to a halt near Ahavath Synagogue's back door. The driver, a tall thin man with short straight dark hair that hung boyishly down over his forehead, wispy goatee, and dead-looking brown eyes, pushed open the driver's door and stepped from the vehicle.

Bruce Carroll Pierce, a member of The Order, looked left and right. Satisfied he was not being watched, Pierce nodded to the man in the passenger seat.

Richard Kemp stepped from the van. Twenty-year-old, six-foot-seven-inch Kemp moved with the uncertainty of a man who did not believe he deserved to take up the space he did. Kemp leaned back into the van and withdrew a two foot section of pipe. He handed the pipe bomb to Pierce, then positioned himself at the back corner of the building so he could watch the street and spot anyone who might happen into the parking lot.

Pierce lowered himself to his haunches and slipped the pipe through the vent located just above the concrete foundation footing.

He bent into his car and grabbed the can of spray paint off the dashboard. After shaking the can, he drew a white swastika on the back of the building. Next to the swastika he spelled out the word, Jewswine.

Pierce tossed the can of paint back into the van. He took a long drag on his cigarette, and held the orange ember to the fuse running from the end of the pipe bomb. He took an extra moment to blow on the end of the fuse to make sure it was smoldering.

"Let's go," Pierce called as he straightened.

He and Kemp jumped quickly back into the van. Pierce popped the transmission lever into drive. He drove rapidly out of the parking lot and turned on to the street, not too fast to draw attention. The last thing they needed was to be stopped for speeding.

They turned another corner and were on their way toward the State Capital when the night sky hemorrhaged orange. A heartbeat later sounded a crashing, glass-shattering explosion. Pierce and Kemp smiled to one another.

"Yahweh, to the mongrel Jews," an excited Pierce said to Kemp. He steered the van toward the safe house, one of several The Order maintained in the Boise area.

The explosion brought people out of the houses adjoining the Synagogue. They were greeted by a great cloud of blue smoke pouring out of the rear of the Ahavath Synagogue. The back of the building was blackened and most of the wall was gone. All the windows in the Synagogue were blown out.

* * *

Lonnie Wilkins was awakened from a deep sleep by noises in front of his north Spokane home.

"What is it?" his wife asked, hearing him stir.

"Nothing," the black man answered, and reached over and patted her bare shoulder. "Go back to sleep."

He slid from bed and made his way silently through the dark house. His instincts warned him against turning on the lights; if there *was* someone outside his house they would be able to see him.

Wilkins reached the living room, stepped to the window, and carefully parted the curtains a few inches. On his lawn not fifteen feet from where he stood were three men in camouflage fatigues. They had just finished sticking the sharpened end of a ten-foot-tall cross wrapped in cloth into the ground. One of the men held a lighter to the bottom of the cross. It ignited with the sound of wind rushing through a small opening. The three men extended their right arms in the stiff-armed Nazi-style salute, then fled to a waiting pickup truck.

The dumfounded black man stood frozen, unable to believe what he just witnessed. His wife approaching from the rear startled him.

"My God," she uttered, and covered her mouth with her hand.

The black couple stared at the burning cross, the fiery glow dancing in their frightened eyes.

* * *

The white girl and her Puerto Rican boyfriend, both sixteen, skated hand-in-hand around the polished hardwood floor of the Coeur d'Alene roller rink. They had been skating for thirty minutes, having such a good time they failed to notice the dirty looks they received from two blond guys in White Power T shirts who skated past them.

The young couple skated fluidly, moving like dancers down the straight-away, until the Puerto Rican boy was blind-sided by one of the guys who had been bad-vibing them. The Puerto Rican boy went sprawling and crashed into the wooden barrier with his shoulder. The boy who cross-checked him stood over him, kicking him in the ribs.

"Miscegenist," the boy snarled while punishing the Puerto Rican boy with the hardened toes of his hockey skates.

"*What are you doing?*" the blond girl screamed, as she skated over to the aid of her boyfriend. "*Are you crazy, or something?*"

She never made it to the wooden barrier. Instead she was pulled down from behind by her long, flaxen hair.

The second boy stood over her, and said, "You are a race traitor, a crime punishable by death. You are ordered to stop fraternizing with the mongrel or you will be dealt with."

The girl, stunned by her fall and by his words, lay perfectly still. She waited until the two boys skated away before picking herself up. She skated slowly and unsteadily over to where her boyfriend was resting on one knee trying to catch his breath.

* * *

It was a warm, beautiful spring day as Larry Broadbent and Bob Hughes strolled lazily along the macadam walkway that followed the shoreline of Lake Coeur d'Alene. Broadbent studied the $20 bill Hughes had just handed him.

"I don't know much about counterfeit money," Broadbent stated. "We usually leave this kind of thing up to you Federal boys..."

"Treasury people tell me it's mediocre," Hughes answered. "Passable if you don't look too close."

"This is the stuff that has been showing up all over the northwest?"

"Also in the east and the Midwest," Hughes explained. "Which lets us know that there are more members of The Order than we first believed. Either that or the same group of guys is driving around the country passing counterfeit money."

"Unbelievable," Broadbent picked up, "that these people are actually in the counterfeiting business to finance an attempt to overthrow the United States government."

"Of course they can't overthrow the government," Hughes added. "But they sure can raise a lot of hell and kill a bunch of innocent people trying. We also figure them to attempt to pull some robberies to raise cash to buy weapons and property."

"Any idea where they're printing this stuff?" Broadbent asked. He held the $20 bill at eye level. Only thing he could find wrong was the blurring of the lines around the White House.

"Somewhere here in the northwest. It'll take awhile but the Treasury boys will find their press."

"You hear Butler filed papers with the state to create what he calls the Nehemiah Township?" Broadbent asked.

Hughes nodded.

"He's proposing that the area around the Aryan Nations compound become an independent township governed by Aryan laws. No people of color or Jews allowed."

"Of course," Hughes emphasized. He took the bill from Broadbent. He turned it over, and pointed to the picture of Andrew Jackson. "They got him looking more like Alfred E. Newman than Andrew Jackson."

"Oh, yeah," Broadbent acknowledged, with a trace of embarrassment that he hadn't caught the flaw.

EIGHT

This was Larry Broadbent's first visit to Spokane, the city of approximately 175,000 situated less than thirty-five miles due west of Coeur d'Alene. Spokane culturally dominated the area; people from Coeur d'Alene felt more a part of Washington State than they did Idaho, whose capital Boise was a grueling eight hour drive down Highway 95, commonly known as the goat trail. People of north Idaho watched Spokane television, read its newspapers, attended Gonzaga or Eastern Washington University, and did their major shopping at one of the malls that ringed the Eastern Washington city.

Larry Broadbent was not, however, traveling to Spokane to shop or attend a college class. He was to visit Rabbi Hyman Gottesman of Temple Beth Shalom.

Temple Beth Shalom was located on a hill on the south side of the city in a handsome modern stone structure whose architecture reminded Broadbent of a medical office building. Broadbent was a little nervous as he knocked on the door of the office, a boxy addition attached to the rear of the synagogue proper. He had never been to a synagogue, nor ever talked with a Rabbi. He had no idea what to expect, maybe an old man with a black hat, beard and long forelocks.

He heard footsteps approach the door from the inside, then nothing. He sensed someone was looking through the peeper at him. The knob turned and the dark wood door was pulled inward. A robust-looking elderly man with bushy gray hair and matching Van Dyke beard stood ready to greet him. Broadbent thought the man looked like an actor in an English car commercial.

"Mr. Broadbent?" asked the man in the dark suit and white shirt open at the throat. "I'm Hyman Gottesman."

"Good of you to see me Rabbi Gottesman," Broadbent answered respectfully.

"Come in, please."

Gottesman led Broadbent to a paneled sitting room furnished with a couch whose brown leather upholstery was attached to the wood frame by brass tacks, and two matching armchairs.

Once they had each settled into an armchair, the Rabbi asked, "What can I do for you?"

"Apparently you haven't seen these." The Undersheriff reached into his inside jacket pocket, removed a flyer, unfolded it and pressed it flat against the coffee table. The flyer showed a caricature of a running black man. Written in large black letters across the bottom half of the paper were the words:

Runnin' Nigger

Move them out of the Northwest,

At the end of a gun if necessary.

Reclaim the country for the white race.

And, at the bottom of the pamphlet.

Temple Beth Shalom.

"In the last couple of days thousands of these have been distributed all over the area, including here in Spokane," Broadbent explained.

Gottesman picked up the flyer. He held it out in front of him and slowly shook his head.

"Of course you don't believe that we are responsible for this garbage."

"No," Broadbent reassured. "We were just wondering if you had any idea who might have printed them."

"Who knows?" the Rabbi answered, his face showing sudden weariness. "There are many people who hate us, who hate blacks, people who would like nothing better than to cause trouble between our two groups."

"I understand," Broadbent said quietly. His system was whispering for a nicotine fix, but he did not feel right asking if he could light up. It was getting more and more difficult to be a smoker, he thought, and smiled grimly to himself.

"There has been a lot of this stuff showing up in the last couple of months," Broadbent picked up. We've even seen posters inviting people to bring live blacks or Asians for target practice at an upcoming gathering at the Aryan Nations compound in Hayden Lake."

Again Rabbi Gottesman shook his head. He looked even more mournful as he said, "The Aryans."

Broadbent nodded.

"Incredible," Gottesman said, pulling at his beard. "This most recent rise in anti-Semitism troubles me greatly. I have received reports this past winter of certain players on a north Idaho high school basketball team with the names of Nazi concentration camps written on their shirts."

"Yeah," Broadbent answered. He felt embarrassed over the

incident. A couple of players on one of Coeur d'Alene's high schools wrote Dachau, Auschwitz and Treblinka on their shirts with a magic marker. The team's coach made the players remove the names of the concentration camps when he became aware of it.

"What can we do to help combat these people and their hateful trash?" the Rabbi asked, angrily tossing the flyer to the coffee table.

"Just tell your people to report any incidents of harassment or anti-Semitism."

"And what would that accomplish?" the Rabbi posed, with a shrug. "Though we have a Malicious Harassment law on the books here in Washington there is no teeth in its enforcement. Anti-Semitism is still treated like a joke.

"If they only realized how it breaks the heart of the victim of racial prejudice. As a Jew you get used to your heart being broken; it happens almost daily," he added, sadly. "It happens in the form of swastikas painted on walls, in the metaphors and jokes about Jews being financial connivers. Then there is the greatest heartbreak of all to my people, this entire industry that has sprung up recently whose only aim is to disprove the occurrence of the Holocaust, this attempt to insinuate that one of the greatest human tragedies of all time is an invention of Jews to elicit sympathy in order to extract payments and political favors for Israel."

Broadbent sat quietly, not knowing what to say.

"And this hate and prejudice will continue to happen, Mr. Broadbent," the Rabbi continued. "Not only to Jews but to other minorities as well. It will continue as long as racism and bigotry are institutionalized in this culture, as long as racism is taught in our schools."

"Taught in the schools?" Broadbent asked.

"How many survivors were there at Little Big Horn?" Gottesman asked, looking intently across the coffee table at Broadbent, a gleam in the Rabbi's otherwise tired, sad eyes.

The Undersheriff scanned his memory. "Two or three?"

A smile showed through the Rabbi's goatee. "What about all of the Indians?"

A flush of discomfort moved up Broadbent's neck. Times like this he wondered how he could possibly be helpful to these people in their struggle against racism and prejudice.

"Try to imagine how a Native American feels each time he or she reads in a history book that Columbus discovered America," Gottesman finished, with a wan smile.

NINE

"This is what we're up against," Dina Tanners said, sliding a recent article from the *Seattle Post-Intelligencer* across the table in the mostly deserted coffee shop.

Larry Broadbent picked up the article. The photograph at the top showed a twenty-foot tall cross blazing against the dark sky. Standing in a circle around the burning cross were about fifty figures, wearing white robes complete with hoods, each with an arm raised in Nazi-style salutes.

Broadbent glanced quickly at the article. Several names were mentioned, including Aryan Nations leader Richard Butler. The article reported that the Aryan Nations had formed an alliance with the Canadian Ku Klux Klan at a recent gathering of white supremacists at the Hayden Lake compound. That gave Broadbent reason to think; he always figured the Klan to be predominately a Southern-U.S.-based organization.

Broadbent passed the article to Rick Morse, seated in the chocolate-brown vinyl booth on the same side of the table as Tanners.

Nine o'clock Wednesday night, Broadbent thought glumly, and I'm sitting in this joint trying to help Tanners and Morse form the Kootenai County Task Force on Human Relations. Broadbent wondered if Sheriff Merf Stalder had made a mistake assigning him to this case. He felt uneducated about the matter of human rights; sometimes, Broadbent thought, Tanners, Morse and the others spoke a different language when they discussed these issues. And still persisting within him to some degree was the old-school-cop philosophy of no crime no perpetrator that wanted to believe that the Aryan Nations were a bunch of kooks who ran around the woods in their camouflage clothes playing soldier. Let them spout all the hate they wanted, as long as they did not act out their ignorant, wacky ideas. And so far, according to everything Broadbent had learned, the Aryans were all talk; the Sheriff's Department had not even been able to tie the Aryan Nations to the defacing of Sid Rosen's restaurant. Further, Butler came out in the press and vehemently denied that his group had had anything to do with painting anti-Semitic slurs on Rosen's restaurant. Even if his people pulled a stunt like that—which they never would, Butler explained—they would be crazy to do it in their own backyard and turn the community against them. Rather than the Aryans defacing Rosen's restaurant, Butler surmised publicly, it was probably the work of Zionists, an effort by Jews to discredit the Aryan Nations.

"Amazing," Rick Morse said, shaking his head as he read the newspaper article. "Butler's group voted to give the Aryan Medal of Honor to Joseph Paul Franklin, that guy who shot and killed those two blacks in Salt Lake City. Listen to what one of the Aryans said about the killings: 'Franklin is a true patriot who loves his people and his culture, and he is being honored for outstanding devotion and courage in line of duty for preservation of race and nation.'

"These people are crazy," Morse finished.

"A bunch of hooligans," Broadbent picked up.

Dina Tanners' dark eyes flashed anger as she looked across the table at Broadbent. "The hooligans of Germany in the 20's became the SS troopers of the 30's. And you can bet that if people like Richard Butler have their way, today's hooligans will be the stormtroopers of fascist America tomorrow. And tomorrow may already be here, given the bombing of the synagogue in Boise."

"We have no proof Butler's people did that."

"You have no proof Butler's people *didn't* do it, either," Tanner challenged.

Broadbent's passive, puppy-dog eyes in no way betrayed his irritation. He was a simple methodical deputy who had been carefully schooled not to give in to the hysterical, emotional frothing of people like Dina Tanners. Broadbent knew from over 20 years as a cop that every story had two sides, and few crimes had implications beyond the lives of those immediately touched by the situation. Tanners' thesis that a handful of north Idaho right-wing extremists might turn into anything akin to German SS troops seemed overblown. He figured the woman was probably given to exaggeration about anti-Semitism because of her people's history of persecution. Tanners as well as the other Jews in Coeur d'Alene were reacting predictably to recent incidents, an understandable knee-jerk defense against anything like the Holocaust ever happening again.

Dina Tanners removed a sheet of paper from her thin butterscotch-colored briefcase. She placed it in the center of the table.

"Here's how I envision the goals of the Task Force," Tanners said, touching each of the four points with the plastic tip of her ballpoint pen as she read. "One, provide support to people victimized by racial and religious harassment. Two, promote legislation that deals with reducing racist activity. Three, provide educational material promoting positive human relations for community use. And, four, monitor racist activity and document incidents."

"Sounds like a lot of work," Broadbent interjected.

"It'll be worth it," the woman countered.

"It's not something we have to do all at once," Morse clarified. "We figure the first one we'll tackle is victim support. Publish our address and phone number in the paper, let people who have been harassed because of their race or religion know there is someone in the community they can talk with. Hopefully, we can assist those who have been victimized file charges against whomever harassed them..."

"If they *want* to file charges," Dina Tanners completed. "Most people will be afraid to step forward."

"All we need is one person willing to press charges," Rick Morse picked up. "By prosecuting the guilty party, the community delivers a message that racist behavior won't be tolerated."

Larry Broadbent leaned back heavily against the vinyl booth. He wanted a cigarette badly, but at Dina Tanners' request they had sat in the non-smoking section.

"Just one Rosa Parks, and we can bring this issue in front of the public," Dina Tanners mused.

Broadbent glanced blankly over at both of them.

Rick Morse smiled with understanding. "She was the black woman in Montgomery, Alabama who refused to give up her seat on the bus to a white man. Her courage was the beginning of the freedom rider movement, and gave the entire civil rights movement a shot in the arm by bringing public awareness to the conditions in which black people lived in the south."

"I see," Broadbent answered. If nothing else, he thought, he was learning about the history of civil rights in this country as a result of his association with these people.

"Do you think this Task Force thing will work?" he asked.

"We don't know," a puzzled-looking Morse said. "It's never been tried before. No community I know of has ever stood up in this fashion to a hate group."

"One of our first jobs," Dina Tanners added, "will be to bring a broad-based group of people into the Task Force. It should be made up of people from every religion and political persuasion. The more non-partisan the Task Force, the more support we'll receive from *all* segments of the community."

"Agreed," Rick Morse said. "I think before the next time we meet each of us should come up with a list of people we'd like to see on the Task Force."

"Sounds good," Dina Tanners finished, and stood. "Another meeting two weeks from today work with both of you?"

"Okay with me," the minister assented.

"Fine by me," Broadbent said, without enthusiasm.

Each dropped a dollar on the table to cover the coffee tab.

Broadbent barely cleared the door when he lit up a cigarette. He opened the door of his car and lowered himself into the seat with a sigh. He paused a moment before driving away. He felt lost doing this kind of community work. Sure it was the way things were done now—cops were no longer just cops; they worked as hard on their community image as they did chasing down criminals—but he still felt like a fish out of water.

Driving away into the night, Broadbent became aware of how exhausted he was. It'd been a long time since 5 o'clock when he awakened for the day, and he was looking forward to watching a little television and crawling into bed. He loved the peace and quiet afforded by the new house he and his wife had purchased in Hayden Lake. The house was his safe, serene spot against all this madness he found himself having to deal with lately.

He allowed his ambivalence about serving on the newly formed Kootenai County Task Force on Human Relations to be nudged aside by the expectation that all this neo-Nazi craziness would calm down and things could get back to normal. If so, maybe he could forget this Task Force business and move on to some meat and potatoes sheriff's work like a robbery or a drug case, even a homicide.

TEN

Eighteen-year-old Scott Wiley rode his bicycle slowly along the sidewalk on an unusually warm February day. Just finished with a game of softball at the school playground with friends, he was on his way home. The tall, wiry Wiley had brown hair, fair skin, and wide, coffee-colored eyes. Scott was Caucasian, unlike his two younger siblings who were mixed race as a result of his mother's union with a black man.

Thinking of all the homework he had to do that night, Wiley rode absentmindedly along the sidewalk. Nearing the end of his senior year in high school, he wanted to graduate with his class. He was ready to get a job.

Concentrating on his running shoes moving up and down on the pedals, Wiley was unaware of the green and white van that eased to the curb. The van crawled along at the same speed Scott traveled.

Scott Wiley glanced towards the street and nearly froze in mid-motion. He had a clear line of vision through the open passenger window of the van, and immediately recognized the man behind the steering wheel. The man with the brown hair and thick mustache was smiling at Wiley in the same sinister way he had a few months before when he had pulled alongside Scott and made racial remarks about Wiley's family. He also fit the description of the man who spit on Scott's five-year-old brother, Lamar, after calling the young boy a race traitor.

"Your life is condemned and you shall be served in front of the devil," Keith Gilbert called from the van, staring hard at Scott Wiley. "You have betrayed your race to conceive niggers and your time shall perish. Thou doest not come forth to my life."

Wiley did not fully understand what the man was saying; nevertheless he realized this weirdo meant him harm. He pedaled faster in hopes the man would leave him alone. Having been on the receiving end of racial slurs before about his family, the boy had never been the victim of a direct threat like this.

The blood left the boy's face and his forehead turned clammy with perspiration. His mouth and throat were a desert.

"How are thee? Thou shalt not live long," Gilbert called. Continuing to glare at the boy in a crazed, sinister way, he maintained the same speed as Scott.

Fear moved through Scott Wiley's body like a charge of electricity. He practically stood his bike on its back tire as he turned for the nearby parking lot. He shot across the macadam, took a short cut through a vacant lot, and headed home. Behind him the green and white van pulled a U-turn, and raced down the street. It swung a right, heading in the opposite direction.

ELEVEN

"We have our Rosa Parks," an excited Dina Tanners said as she pushed into Larry Broadbent's office.

Broadbent glanced up from behind his desk. This was the first time he had not seen Dina Tanners intensely serious; now she was intensely excited. He figured she was giving off enough energy to light a good-sized house.

"What do you mean?" he asked. Index cards in his mind flipped over until the right one came up and he recalled Rosa Parks.

"A woman whose children have been racially harassed is willing to file a complaint against the Aryans!"

Broadbent's blood raced. This was the one they were waiting for. In the past few weeks, since the Task Force had installed its telephone hotline, they had received a number of complaints from people who had been harassed because of their skin color or religious beliefs. None, however, had been willing to press charges out of fear of reprisal from the Aryans.

"Her name is Connie Fort, and she's due at Dana Wetzel's office any time now," Tanners explained. "I'm on my way over there. Want to go?"

"Sure." Broadbent stood and followed the woman out of his office.

The Tanners woman rode with Broadbent a dozen or so blocks to City Hall. They hustled into the recently constructed building, past Dana Wetzel's secretary, into the Coeur d'Alene City Prosecutor's neat, well lit office.

Dana Wetzel was seated at a small conference table. In her late 30's, she was known around the legal community as a scrappy prosecutor and an articulate consensus-builder. She had shoulder-length blond hair, square shoulders, medium frame, and pleasant features. As Broadbent had only recently learned, she was part Native American, which explained the fervor with which she went after those who discriminated against minorities.

Across the table from Wetzel was a thin worried-looking woman with washed out blond hair. Broadbent guessed her to be about the same age as the city prosecutor. Unlike Wetzel, who wore a stylish blue suit and white chiffon shirt, the other woman was dressed in jeans, gray sweatshirt and running shoes. Seated next to the woman was Scott Wiley.

Dana Wetzel stood to greet Broadbent and Dina Tanners. The city prosecutor in turn introduced Broadbent and Tanners to Scott Wiley, and to his mother, Connie Fort.

"I waited until you got here to have Ms. Fort tell her story," Wetzel explained. "I wanted you to hear it firsthand."

Broadbent and Tanners joined Dana Wetzel, Connie Fort and Scott Wiley at the small conference table.

"Please, go ahead," Dana Wetzel suggested, gently.

Connie Fort attempted to talk, but her chin began trembling and emotion robbed her voice. She reached into her purse for a tissue, and wiped her nose, red and raw from crying.

"It began in February of this year..." she started, in the heavy accent of her native Netherlands.

"No, mom," Scott Wiley cut in. "You're forgetting what happened to Lamar last July."

"You're right," the Fort woman acknowledged. She pressed her hands against her temples, trying to compose herself. "It began last July, I think it was the 12th, when this man walked up to my youngest son, who was then five, and called him a race traitor. Then he spit on him."

Something about the image of a grown man spitting on a five-year-old boy caused Larry Broadbent to clench his jaw.

"I didn't go to the police then," the woman explained, "because I didn't want to drag a boy that young through a court proceeding. Plus, I was scared."

Broadbent glanced across the table at Dina Tanners. Her eyes shone like polished marbles.

"Then there was the incident in February." Connie Fort picked up. Her shoulders shook with stifled sobs, as she dabbed at her nose and eyes with her handkerchief. She glanced questioningly at her son.

"That's right, Mom," the boy confirmed. "It was February 23rd."

"Why don't you tell it, Scott," the woman suggested, thoughtfully. "You know the details better than I do."

Scott Wiley's face grew pale, and he tugged at the collar of his shirt.

Broadbent studied the boy. He saw the fear move through Scott's body like a fever. Broadbent figured the incident must have scared the boy half to death.

Scott Wiley recounted the two incidents in which the person in the green and white van had threatened him because his mother had borne two mixed-race children.

Larry Broadbent looked instinctively towards Dana Wetzel.

The city prosecutor returned his glance, and explained, "His name is Keith Gilbert. He's a member of something called the Social Nationalist Aryan People's Party. This is the same guy who has been identified over the past year as harassing black and Asian students at North Idaho College."

Broadbent nodded, and turned back to Connie Fort. The woman was slowly shaking her head while crying so hard her entire upper body shook. Dina Tanners reached over and placed her hand gently on Fort's shoulder.

Larry Broadbent felt a deep sense of rage and disgust, along with sadness, that the Wiley boy had been subjected to the brand of hate Keith Gilbert had leveled towards him. Broadbent also respected Scott enormously for having the courage to speak the truth despite being so afraid.

"Why didn't you report the February incident to the police?" Broadbent asked Connie Fort.

"I did."

Broadbent looked at Wetzel.

"Apparently the investigating officer didn't judge the problem to be a serious one," the city prosecutor reported. A sheepish look on her face tipped that she had a hand in that decision and was now regretting it. "Plus, we had no witnesses."

Wetzel handed a copy of the police incident report to Broadbent. The Undersheriff read quickly through it. Then he looked up at

Connie Fort, who seemed more angry now than sorrowful or fearful.

"Are you and your son prepared to go through a jury trial on this?" Dana Wetzel asked.

"Yes," the woman said, resolutely.

"It'll be a difficult case to pursue," Wetzel added. "There was no physical contact associated with the threat to your son. Only a verbal threat."

"I understand that," the Fort woman answered.

Wetzel turned to Broadbent. "I believe what Keith Gilbert did is against the law. He frightened this boy terribly with his threats."

Broadbent nodded his agreement.

"And there's more," Wetzel revealed.

Broadbent's right eyebrow arched in anticipation.

"Ms. Fort, tell Undersheriff Broadbent what you discussed with me earlier," Dana Wetzel pursued, turning to the blond woman.

Fear pushed back into Connie Fort's face.

"The phone calls started about the time that Keith Gilbert threatened Scott," the woman recounted. "They usually came late at night. Whomever was on the other end—it was always a man— called me a race traitor, a miscegenist, and said I was guilty of race treason. He threatened me with execution by public hanging."

She began trembling so hard she could not speak. She dabbed at her nose with her handkerchief.

While Fort was trying to compose herself, Dana Wetzel added, "Ms. Fort received these in the mail."

Broadbent studied the flyers Wetzel handed him. One was entitled, "Race Traitors." It threatened anyone who fraternized socially or sexually with blacks with a trial, and, if found guilty, execution. Negroes who fraternized with whites would be executed on the spot.

The second sheet was the *Runnin' Nigger* poster distributed recently around north Idaho and eastern Washington. The third flyer was most disturbing of all to Broadbent. A photo copy of a small newspaper article from the *Seattle Times* was centered in the middle of the page. Below the article was the Aryan Nations swastika. The newspaper article explained that the police had found a partially decomposed body of an unidentified black man in Sprague Lake, located about 15 miles southeast of Spokane. The man had been killed by a bullet to the head. The authorities were requesting anyone with information about the man's identity or circumstances of his death to contact them.

A disgusted and angry Larry Broadbent shook his head. He had no use for a bully that would harass and intimidate a single mother and her children for the only reason that her two boys were mixed-race. What sort of man would threaten Scott Wiley with murder, or spit on Wiley's five-year-old brother? The Undersheriff was looking forward to meeting this Keith Gilbert character.

Dina Tanners broke the silence in the room. "I want you to know, Ms. Wetzel, that the Task Force will do everything we can to help you try this case. We are at your disposal."

"That's right," Larry Broadbent heard himself saying, with a conviction he had not felt up to this moment about this business of human rights.

TWELVE

No matter how many times he had done so in the past, Larry Broadbent always got the jitters before testifying in court; his stomach felt as if he was in an airplane in a quick descent. Attempting to distract his mind, he leaned back against the wooden bench-seat and studied the other people in the courtroom. His gaze fell on Scott Wiley, seated in the first row behind the prosecutor's table, where Dana Wetzel was arranging some papers. Next to Wiley were Connie Fort, Dina Tanners and Rick Morse. One of them from time to time leaned over to whisper words of encouragement to Scott.

At the defense table sat Keith Gilbert. Longish brown hair combed neatly to one side, Gilbert projected an air of detached arrogance. Next to Gilbert was his attorney, David Manko. Occupying the first two rows of seats behind Gilbert was a contingent of men in camouflage fatigues. Each of these men had off and on, throughout the proceeding, glowered menacingly at Scott Wiley.

Wiley was holding up well, both on the witness stand and while seated next to his mother. He refused to be intimidated by Gilbert, or by the group of Aryans.

The boy testified that Keith Gilbert pulled over in his van and harassed him as he was returning home from a neighborhood softball game. Scott also related about the earlier incident in which Gilbert pulled up next to him in his van and threatened him.

Connie Fort also testified in a tearful yet determined fashion about how she tried to console Scott and her other son, who was spit on by a man matching Gilbert's description.

Equally damaging testimony against Gilbert came from two students from Gonzaga University in Spokane, who over the past few months traveled to the Aryan Nations compound several times to conduct interviews for a school project. These two students, brought to the prosecutor's attention by Dina Tanners and Rick Morse of the Task Force, overheard Gilbert bragging to other members of the Aryan Nations about harassing Scott Wiley while the boy was riding home on his bicycle from the softball game.

"The court calls Larry Broadbent to the stand," the bailiff announced, bringing the Undersheriff out of his thoughts.

Broadbent pushed to his feet, and took a second to arrange the front of his blue suit jacket. Proceeding up the aisle, he glanced at the jury, composed of six Kootenai County residents. They would decide if Keith Gilbert was guilty of two counts of verbal assault, one count for each of the two incidents. Broadbent, along with everyone in the room, knew this had the makings of a historic case; this was the first time in Idaho that a case was tried under the State's verbal assault statute; and Idaho was one of only two states—Florida being the other—with such a law on the books.

City Prosecutor Dana Wetzel asked him a few routine questions about the incident and about the charge brought against Gilbert. After Wetzel completed direct examination of Broadbent, she returned to her seat. Broadbent looked to his right, to the defense table. Keith Gilbert's attorney, readying to stand to question Broadbent, was stopped by Gilbert, who reached up and caught him by the crook of the arm. Gilbert whispered into the bushy-haired man's ear, then turned a look on Broadbent meant to cook the flesh off his bones.

The defense lawyer stepped over to face Broadbent. The Undersheriff had seen David Manko around the courthouse a few times, but had never spoken to him.

"Your honor," Manko said, "I only have one question for Mr. Broadbent."

Broadbent was relieved. He did not like being on the hot seat, and wanted this over as quickly as possible. Whenever called on to testify, he was always tortured by the fear he might say something dumb and damage the prosecutor's case.

"Undersheriff Broadbent," the defense attorney posed. He leaned his elbow on one corner of the witness box and looked respectfully at the Undersheriff, as if preparing to engage in a pleasant conversation over coffee with an old friend. "Though I don't believe for a second he did, let's for the moment pretend that my client, Mr. Keith Gilbert, actually did say those things to the Wiley boy. If that were true, Undersheriff Broadbent, wouldn't you say that this was a nuisance case not worthy of the court's time. I mean if we tried every person who yelled something from a car at another citizen wouldn't we have the courts packed with a lot of nonsensical, annoyance suits that would add to what is already a *very* litigious society?"

Broadbent glanced to his right before answering. Gilbert and the dozen or so Aryans were drilling holes through Broadbent with their eyes. The Undersheriff shifted his gaze to Scott Wiley. The boy, chin on his palm, waited expectantly for Broadbent to respond. Connie Fort, startled expression on her face, also waited.

Larry Broadbent turned to the defense attorney, and looked the pudgy man square in the eyes.

"A few months ago I might've thought this kind of thing was, as you said, an annoyance suit," Broadbent began. "Believe me I have a lot of other things I'd rather be doing than spending two days in court. But the events that have taken place around here over the past few months have changed my mind. Coming to understand how much fear and shame Mr. Gilbert heaped on Scott Wiley—whose only crime, even according to Gilbert himself, is that he's from a mixed-race family—has convinced me that Mr. Keith Gilbert should stand trial for what he did...

"No," Broadbent completed, his eyes fixed solidly on David Manko's, "I don't think this is a nuisance suit."

"Your honor, I move to strike Undersheriff Broadbent's answer, because it was not responsive to my question," the defense attorney interjected.

"Sustained," the youngish, dark-haired judge determined.

"Sorry," Larry Broadbent acknowledged. Inside he felt good that maybe his comments helped fix Gilbert's guilt in the jury's mind.

Larry Broadbent felt light on his feet as he left the witness box. He stepped briskly across the front of the court and headed down the aisle towards the rear section of the room. On his way he heard whispering from his right, the area in which the group of Aryans were seated.

"Nigger lover," one of them said, loud enough for Broadbent and many in the front of the room—including Scott Wiley and Connie Fort—to hear.

"Race traitor," hissed another.

"Yahweh to you and your race-traitor family," said another.

Yahweh? Broadbent thought. I'll have to ask Tanner and the others what *that* means.

Broadbent turned out to be the final witness; the defense attorney surprised everyone by not putting his client on the stand.

While the judge charged the jury, Broadbent glanced at Keith Gilbert. The defendant sat with his upper body twisted slightly to his right, glowering at Broadbent.

Afterwards the Undersheriff stepped out into the hall for a smoke. He had breathed up about half of the cigarette when Dina Tanners approached him.

"What do you think they'll do?" she asked, leaning away from the aura of blue smoke encircling Broadbent.

"Tough to say."

"It'll take a lot of courage for them to come back with a guilty verdict," she answered.

Broadbent nodded his agreement. This was a small town, and the people on the jury knew that sooner or later they would run into one of the members of the Aryan Nations on the street. Or worse, they could be paid a visit by the burly men in camouflage fatigues.

"I hope that, if nothing else," Broadbent ventured, "this proceeding sends out a signal to the community that the system will protect them from the likes of the Aryans."

"That's what we're all counting on," Tanners agreed.

"I need to go over to my office and take care of some things," Broadbent explained, before snuffing his cigarette into the sand-filled ashtray.

Broadbent left the courthouse, stepped next door to the Sheriff's office, and climbed the stairs to the second floor. Once in his office he phoned the bailiff and instructed him to ring him when the jury was ready to come back. He then turned his attention to paperwork.

Before he knew it, three hours had passed and the phone on his desk was jangling. It was the bailiff. The jury was on its way back into the courtroom.

All in one motion Broadbent butted out his cigarette and bolted for the door. He made it to the courtroom just as the lean, small and befuddled-looking jury foreman was readying to announce the verdict.

"The jury finds the defendant Keith Gilbert not-guilty of the first count of verbal assault..."

Broadbent's heart sank. He looked at the defense table. Gilbert was smiling. At the other side of the room, Scott Wiley's face was ashen. Connie Fort had her head in her hands.

"...We find the defendant, Keith Gilbert," the jury foreman continued, trying his best to fix his watery eyes on Gilbert, "guilty on the second count of verbal assault."

"All *right*," Broadbent said to himself, and socked his palm. By delivering this verdict the people of north Idaho said that race-based harassment was unacceptable.

Broadbent realized that the conviction also did a lot to empower Dina Tanners and Rick Morse in their efforts to pull together the Kootenai County Task Force on Human Relations. Despite the important work of Tanners and Morse in helping the prosecutor assemble the case against Keith Gilbert, the Task Force was still in its infancy. The publicity generated by this case, a recent article in the paper written by Dina Tanners about the goals of the newly formed Task Force, and now this conviction, were going to give the Task Force immense credibility. Already Dina Tanners had received calls from various members of the community—some well known, others regular citizens—who wanted to serve on the Task Force.

Broadbent's attention was drawn back to the proceedings. The defense attorney, acting on Gilbert's orders, waived the customary delay until sentencing. The judge called Gilbert to the front of the bench.

"Mr. Gilbert," the judge asked, "do you have anything to say before I pass sentencing?"

His hard, cold eyes fixed on the judge, Gilbert extended his right arm in the Nazi-style salute.

"I pledge myself to an all-white homeland and to the principle of a territorial imperative," Gilbert recited, his voice carrying to the back of the room. "Long live Nehemiah Township!"

Each man seated behind Keith Gilbert jumped to his feet, and raised his arm in the Nazi salute.

"Mr. Keith Gilbert," the judge picked up, his eyes on the papers in front of him as he appeared to ignore the defendant's action of standing with his right arm extended. "You have been found guilty of Section 18-901B of the Idaho State Penal Code, a misdemeanor. I hereby sentence you to a fifty dollar fine, plus seventy-five days in the county jail, sentence to begin immediately."

Gasps rose from the fifty or so people in the courtroom. The sentence was much stiffer than anyone expected. It was one of the harshest ever handed down in Kootenai County for a misdemeanor assault conviction.

Gilbert's expression remain unchanged. One of the Aryans behind him called, "Yahweh to you, judge of the ZOG Jewocracy."

While the bailiff approached him, Keith Gilbert sneered openly at the judge. The bailiff led Gilbert through the door to the left of the bench, into the corridor that connected the courtroom to the jail.

Broadbent waited for the exhausted-looking Dana Wetzel to make her way past well-wishers, to the back of the courtroom.

"Good job, prosecutor," Broadbent said, and patted the woman lightly on the shoulder.

"Appreciate it," Wetzel answered, pushing her hair out of her eyes.

"This should stop some of that Aryan Nations nonsense."

"Let's hope so," Wetzel added. "At least they know that the people won't be intimidated into not pressing charges."

"Too bad the crime wasn't a felony so the sentence could be a little stiffer," Broadbent added.

Larry Broadbent lit a cigarette, as the two of them paused in the corridor to watch the contingent of Aryans push brusquely out of the courtroom. As the group of men in camouflage fatigues walked past him and Dana Wetzel, Broadbent had the sense he was in the presence of a simmering evil.

"What do you think we'll hear from the Aryans because of this trial?" Wetzel asked, once the men in fatigues had left the courthouse.

"No way of knowing. However, I'm certain things are going to get a little hotter for them from now on. I heard from the FBI a couple of days ago. They picked up news of this case on the Associated Press wire and have begun an investigation of Richard Butler and the Aryan Nations. Mr. Gilbert may have cost his band of hatemongers more than they realize."

Broadbent consumed most of his cigarette in one long pull.

"Let's hope if the FBI finds anything they'll move faster than we did," Wetzel summed up. "We'd been receiving reports of incidents of harassment for over a year before we were able to prosecute one of them."

"My guess is that this case, and now the FBI involvement, will about finish the Aryans Nations," Broadbent mused. "They know they're being watched."

"I think you're probably right. I have to go."

Larry Broadbent, watching the prosecutor walk away, butted out his cigarette, and moved off in the direction of the doorway into the Sheriff's building. As he went, he wondered if his statement about the Aryan Nations being finished was based on fact or magical thinking.

THIRTEEN

Aryan Nations Compound

Charlotte Bray swept around the lectern of the chapel. She wore her honey-colored hair gathered in back, and a red and black bandanna to keep the dust off her head, along with a denim shirt, jeans, and running shoes. She did a fast thorough job of sweeping, then took a mop to the area, leaving it spotless.

Taking pride in her work, along with a fear of God, was something taught by her parents on the Minnesota dairy farm on which she was raised. Charlotte considered the strict religious training she received from her parents a good foundation for life; no matter what happened around her, the woman was able to focus her mind and body on the task at hand while maintaining a strong contact with God. "Don't mentally resist what you're doing physically," her father always said. "That way you'll be able to face life's problems and have plenty of energy left over to do God's work." Over the past few years God's work had been tough, culminating in the loss of the 80 acre dairy farm that had been in her family four generations.

Finished cleaning the chapel, Charlotte placed the broom, dustpan, mop and bucket in the small maintenance room at the rear of the building. She stepped through the door marked "Ladies Room," and quickly washed up. There was another job to perform, this one very different from the one she had just completed.

As head of the welcoming committee, it fell to Charlotte Bray to greet newcomers to the Aryan Nations compound. Recently the number of people moving to north Idaho to join the white supremacist movement was on the increase. Today there was a family arriving from Wisconsin.

Under the watchful eye of the guard in the nearby tower, Charlotte walked across the grassy area rimmed by the compound's buildings. She stepped into the office, where she was greeted by Betty Tate. Tate was seated at her desk, composing a letter on her electric typewriter.

"Hi, Charlotte," Betty Tate greeted. Like Charlotte, Tate was blond and sturdily built. She had inquisitive green eyes, a broad nose, and a small, soft mouth.

"What time are those folks from Wisconsin supposed to get here?" Bray inquired.

Betty glanced at her wristwatch. "Anytime, now... somewhere around four o'clock."

"Mind if I wait here?"

"Of course not," Betty Tate responded, pleasantly. "You want anything... Coffee?"

"No, thanks."

Betty Tate opened a manila folder, and quickly read the handwritten letter. "Says here that they have one child, a thirteen year old boy. I asked my son, David, to stop by after school so he can help the boy feel at home."

Charlotte Bray smiled, remembering how welcome she and her family had felt the day they arrived at the compound, two years earlier. She and her husband were frightened and demoralized. Everything had been taken from them: their farm, their optimism and innocence, and most of their self-esteem. But all that changed since arriving at the Aryan compound. Reverend Butler helped them believe in themselves once again; he showed them how to put the events of the past few years into a spiritual and historical perspective. Further, Butler helped Charlotte Bray and her husband understand that unless they were willing to fight for their country they would lose it. The white race was on the way to becoming a minority in this white Christian country. People like Charlotte Bray were being forgotten by the very government that was supposed to represent them.

"If you don't mind, Char, I have to get this letter done this afternoon..." Betty Tate said, glancing down at her typewriter.

"Go ahead." Charlotte sat quietly while Tate turned back to her work.

Ten minutes later a decade-old maroon Ford pickup truck with a terminal case of rust and mud-spattered Wisconsin plates pulled up in front of the office. A stocky, dark-haired man pushed from the cab. Waiting in the truck was a tired and confused-looking brunette woman, and a dark-haired boy with suspicious dark eyes and a puffy face.

Charlotte smiled to herself as she watched the man walk gingerly toward the office door. They all have that same distrustful, scared look, she thought. By the time they get here, Bray mused, they are seriously questioning the sanity of their decision to cut everything loose and move to north Idaho. That all changes, however, once they talk with other members of the Aryan Nations and meet Reverend Butler. Most of them decide to stay, almost unanimously stating the same thing, that they felt as though by moving to north Idaho they had come home and that Reverend Butler was heaven-sent.

"Name's Nick Morrison," the man said, his dark eyes working the place over.

"I'm Charlotte Bray. And this is Betty Tate."

Morrison dipped his weathered face towards the two women. He had a two-day growth of beard, and his hair was crazed and oily.

Charlotte figured he drove straight through to save money.

"Let's step over to the dining hall for a cup of coffee," Charlotte suggested. "Bring your family along. Bet we could arrange for a couple of pieces of hot apple pie."

Morrison's eyes brightened as he turned on the heel of his work boot toward his truck.

"I'll let Mr. Morrison know that Reverend Butler will see him later," Charlotte informed Betty Tate.

"Good," Tate responded.

Bray stepped into the long shadows cast by the afternoon sun. She approached the passenger side of the truck and extended her hand.

"Hi. I'm Charlotte Bray. Welcome."

The thin brunette woman wiped her hand on her denim pant leg before offering it to Bray. "I'm Nancy. This is our son, Dennis."

A miniature version of his father, Dennis nodded respectfully.

"C'mon, I'll show you around," Charlotte said, warmly.

They started in the direction of the dining hall, but were headed off by David, Betty Tate's son. The blond, blue-eyed boy wore the standard Aryan garb of well-polished black boots and camouflage pants and shirt. His overly-serious rigid look belied his sixteen years.

"Hi, you must be Dennis," David said, and fell into step with the Morrison boy.

Dennis looked at his father as if seeking permission to speak with the other boy. He turned his eyes back on David. "Yeah. I'm Dennis."

"I'm David Tate. I live here on the compound."

"How long have you lived here?" the Morrison boy asked.

"Almost ten years. Ever since Reverend Butler moved his church here."

"How about school?" Dennis asked.

"We have school here."

That pleased the Morrison boy.

Charlotte led the group into the dining hall, a narrow building on whose beige, polished vinyl tile floor were a dozen round tables ringed by folding chairs. At the far end was a well-equipped kitchen, heavy on the stainless steel.

"Please, sit down," Charlotte said and motioned toward the table closest to the door. "I'll get us some coffee and pie... David, why don't you get Dennis what he wants."

"I'll have milk, and pie," the Morrison boy picked up, hesitantly.

Charlotte glanced knowingly at the boy. Most of them come here like that, she thought; hesitant and cowed by their parents misery.

"I'll bet he'd like some ice cream on his pie, too," Bray added.

David followed Charlotte into the kitchen. The Tate boy filled two glasses of milk from the machine, then fixed two apple pies à la mode, all with a well-practiced efficiency.

"After you finish your pie, David," Charlotte said, "you can show Dennis around the property. He might like to see the stream out back. I haven't met a boy yet who doesn't like to fish."

"Yes, ma'am," the Tate boy answered. He placed the dishes and glasses on a tray, and walked lightly to the dining area.

Charlotte Bray prepared a tray of fresh coffee and pie à la mode for herself and the Morrisons, then followed David into the dining room. She served Nick and Nancy Morrison.

"C'mon outside," David Tate said, after he and Dennis wolfed down their pie and milk. "I'll show you around."

Again the Morrison boy looked to his father for permission.

"Go ahead," Nick Morrison said. "Have fun."

Once the two boys were out of the room, Charlotte Bray turned to the Morrisons.

"I'll be happy to answer any questions you might have about the Church of Jesus Christ Christian," she began.

Nancy and Nick Morrison looked at one another.

"How did you come to hear about Reverend Butler's work?" Charlotte asked, trying to get things started.

"A friend at the paper mill used to receive Reverend Butler's newsletter," Nick Morrison explained. "I got to reading it, but didn't connect much with what Reverend Butler was saying until the paper mill closed down and I was out of a job."

Charlotte nodded. It was a story she had heard many times before; it was her family's story.

"Some goddamned Jap corporation bought out the company, closed the plant down with one day's notice," Morrison continued.

His jaw jumped, his eyes were drawn tight, and he watched his strong, wide hands clasped on the table in front of him. "One day's notice. Unknown to any of us, they had built a new mill in Japan. Twenty-six years I was with the company, and I get tossed aside like an old sock."

Large tears appeared on Nancy Morrison's bottom lids. "We couldn't afford health insurance. Then Dennis got sick, and needed surgery. It wiped us out. We lost everything. Our savings, house, everything."

"The mill was the only industry in the town," Nick Morrison picked up, his eyes glittering. "I tried to get on somewhere else, but I'm the wrong color."

"He tried everywhere," Nancy Morrison revealed, her mouth bunched tight and colorless, like cauliflower. "What jobs there was in our area were given to blacks under that damned Affirmative Action program."

"It was about the time when we had to move in with Nancy's parents that the stuff I'd read about us whites losing our own country began to make sense," Nick Morrison completed. "Everything Reverend Butler said about the white race needing to stick together started to click. We decided to come out here and help start the Aryan all-white homeland."

"We're glad you're here," Charlotte offered, gently. She reached out and patted Nancy Morrison's forearm.

Nick Morrison took a long pull of coffee, and squared his shoulders.

"How much does it cost to stay here?" the Morrison man asked, with difficulty. "We don't have much left."

"There is no cost," Charlotte Bray answered, softly. "Reverend Butler has chosen as his ministry to aid white people in every way he can. All we ask is that once you get work you donate what you can to the movement."

A look of relief swept over Nancy Morrison's face. "We'll do all we can to help out around here until Nick gets a job and we can pay our way."

"We appreciate that," Charlotte completed.

"What *is* the work situation in the area?" Nick Morrison asked.

"We can help you get a job," Charlotte Bray answered, with a confidence that impressed the Morrison man. "We have friends in the community."

A look of relief washed over Morrison's face. He tenderly placed his hand over his wife's slender, white one.

"In the meantime, why don't you take a few days to get to know the area," Bray continued. "North Idaho is very beautiful. There will be plenty of time to work."

They were interrupted when an excited Dennis Morrison pushed through the door into the dining hall. Right behind him was David Tate.

"Mom! Dad!" Dennis blurted, his face glowing. "There's so much to do here!! David said he'd take me to the firing range and target practice with him."

"That's fine, son," Nick Morrison said, a smile playing on his lips.

Charlotte Bray leaned back in her seat. She felt good that the

Morrisons liked it here; that meant she was doing her job well.

"When do we get to meet Reverend Butler?" Nancy Morrison asked.

"Tonight, after seven o'clock church service. Reverend Butler has scheduled a reception in your honor."

Nancy Morrison's face lit up with pleasure.

"In the meantime," Charlotte added, "we better get you situated. You'd probably like to get unpacked and cleaned up before dinner."

Nick Morrison pushed wearily to his feet.

"Dad," Dennis Morrison interjected, "Can I go target shooting with David?"

"Maybe later, son," Nick Morrison answered. "Right now you have to help us get settled."

Though obviously disappointed, the Morrison boy said no more about it. Charlotte Bray liked the way Morrison controlled his son. Authority over one's family was a highly valued virtue in the Aryan Nations compound.

"I'll come by later, after you've unpacked," David assured. "We have a lot of time to spend together."

"C'mon," Charlotte said, "I'll show you to your cabin."

FOURTEEN

The stocky man leaned over the printing press and worked the long screwdriver into the guts of the motor, grunting and cursing with his effort. The printing press was a good one, a workhorse, for which the Aryan Nations had paid several thousand dollars a couple of years back.

Walter West stepped away from the press. He blotted sweat from his forehead on the sleeve of his shirt, which he wore rolled to the elbow. The dark, thick hair on his forearms was matted with perspiration and grease.

West reached for the styrofoam cup on the nearby counter and took a long swig of whiskey. Swishing the whiskey around in his mouth like mouthwash, he glanced at his wristwatch. Quarter of two in the morning. Everything went well, he figured, he ought to have the printing press back in operation by eight o'clock when Reverend Butler and Betty Tate arrived for work. A big printing job needed to be completed within the next couple of days; they needed to have this press working.

West took another swallow of whiskey, and briefly gave some thought to all the work that lay in front of him over the next few days. He was not likely to get any sleep tonight, plus he would be on his feet most of tomorrow preparing orders for mailing. Tomorrow night, he, Bob Merki, David Tate and Gary Yarbrough were slated to spend the night printing green, the counterfeit money The Order needed to purchase weapons. Lack of sleep, however, did not bother

West. Everything he was doing was for a good cause, the most important one there was.

He decided to take five, and lit a cigarette. While dragging on the cigarette, West let his mind travel back three years, to when he arrived at the Aryan Nations compound. He remembered how amazed he was upon coming to work in the print shop at the amount of material Richard Butler mailed out every week to those who requested it. West had had no idea there were that many people out there who believed as he did, that the white race was in danger of losing control of the United States to the kikes, niggers, spics and other mongrel races.

West learned about the movement while working in a tool and die shop in California, a medium-sized plant that did contract work for the aerospace industry. He was there nearly four years when he began noticing that whenever someone lost their job at the plant, that person was replaced by a black, Asian or Hispanic. West asked around and learned the company was hiring minorities to comply with the federal government's Affirmative Action program. That really ticked him off; he complained to anyone who listened about people of color getting preference over whites when it came to hiring. It was about that time that one of the guys in the plant gave him the Aryan Nations literature. The authors of the pamphlets—Richard Butler, Robert Miles and others—had set down in words exactly what West believed for some time was wrong with this country.

He immediately wrote Richard Butler and advised him that he was taking the Aryan Nations leader up on his offer to move to north Idaho. Once here, West never left the compound. As far as he was concerned, being here with his people, and working for the cause of a white homeland, was like living in Eden. Furthermore, Walter West felt needed and important. He possessed skills that were in demand around the Aryan Nations compound, and Reverend Butler looked after all his worldly needs. Living, working and worshipping with his own kind made Walter West happier than ever before.

The only area of his life that was not going well, however, was his marriage. He and Sue argued a lot lately, mostly about his drinking. Damn woman, he thought, making a federal case out of a guy having a few drinks. Worse, the last time he beat her she checked into a battered women's shelter for a week. He eventually talked her into coming back; she knew where she belonged and who was boss of their house.

West set the styrofoam cup down, placed the cigarette between his lips, and returned to working on the press. He popped the cover off the motor; he had an idea the trouble might be a burned out contact.

He heard the door open behind him. Arms still in the press, he turned his head.

"Up late, aren't you, Randy?" he asked.

"We have some business to take care of," the rangy, muscular and balding Randy Duey stated. "We're going to need your help on this one."

West pulled his arms out of the press and reached for the rag draped over the paper-cutter. He wiped grease off his hands and forearms.

"Sure thing," West answered. In the Aryan Nations you did not refuse a request of one of your superiors.

Randy Duey turned for the door, Walter West right behind.

Once outside, Duey instructed, "This way."

Duey, in jeans and tan shirt open at the throat, pointed at the decade-old red Ford sedan parked in back of the print shop.

Walter West followed Randy Duey to the car. West opened the door and climbed into the passenger seat. He was momentarily startled upon noticing the tall, thin man sitting in the back seat.

"Dick... Hi!" West greeted, turning to Richard Kemp.

"Hi, Walter."

Duey sat behind the wheel, turned the starter, and without the benefit of headlights eased out of the quiet compound. His eyes set behind thick rimless glasses, Duey drove by moonlight down the dirt road, past the guard's booth, to the highway. About a mile down the highway he turned on the headlights.

West settled into the front seat; he knew better than to ask where they were headed. Being an Aryan warrior meant dealing in secrecy.

They kept to the back roads and drove nearly two hours. West figured they were somewhere north of Priest Lake, in wild, wooded and sparsely populated country.

Duey turned off the pavement, and steered down a pockmarked dirt logging road into woods so dense the trees and underbrush along the road was a solid wall. They pulled to a stop in back of another vehicle, a small foreign-model pickup truck.

"Here we are," Duey said, and killed the car lights. It was pitch-black-dark; the forest was so thick the moon was unable to find the forest floor.

All three men got out of the car.

Walter West took a moment to stretch. Three hours bending over the printing press, and another two riding in the car had taken its toll on his back. He breathed deeply of the pine-scented air, locked his hands behind his neck, and bent forward. He was into his stretch when he was struck savagely in the back of the head with a ballpeen hammer by Richard Kemp.

West fell forward, his face smacking against the hard gravel. He was stunned but still conscious.

Next he heard the faint click of a gun's hammer.

He turned his bloody head quickly around, and stared into the menacing snout of a .357 Magnum.

"Wha..? What's this all about?"

"You talk too much, Walter. One of these days you're gonna say something to the wrong person," Randy Duey said, with a cool, detached rage.

"And you beat your wife."

Blood running down the back of his neck, West thought about running but decided instead to attempt to talk them out of it.

"I haven't been talking with anyone..."

"You're lying," Duey interrupted. He leveled the gun on West's face. "Goodbye, Walter. I'm sorry. We can't let you ruin it for everyone."

"*No, no,*" West screamed, and instinctively turned away. "You got it all wrong."

The last thing Walter West felt was the cold steel gun barrel pressing against his skull behind his ear. There was a roar of a gun blast, and Walter West's lights went out.

"Damn," sounded the excited voice. "Did you see that? The top of his head came off."

Two other men stepped out of the darkness, to the logging road. They each carried a long-handled, pointed shovel. In the bed of the pickup was a bag of lye.

"Bury him deep so the animals don't dig him up before the lye does its work," Randy instructed.

The two men carrying the shovels walked a few paces off the abandoned logging road, and began digging in the rocky soil. The younger one, David Tate, returned to help drag Walter West's body to the grave. Tate noticed West's brains spread all over the logging road It looked as though someone had thrown a bucket of macaroni on the ground. David Tate turned away and vomited.

FIFTEEN

Seated behind his desk, Marshall Mend stared at the headlines that blared across the top of the newspaper: ORDER LEADER ROBERT MATHEWS KILLED IN FIERY WHIDBEY ISLAND SHOOTOUT. The sub-heading explained that Mathews died at the end of a two day shoot-out with over 200 federal agents on the island in Washington's Puget Sound.

"Damn," Mend said. He balanced the newspaper on the tips of his fingers as if trying to assess by its weight how badly the publicity was going to damage not only his real estate business but his new hometown as well. "This is all we need."

Over the past few months The Order had been major news in the local, national and international media. Each time one of its exploits was detailed in a newspaper, magazine, or on radio or television, the reporter mentioned that the members of The Order had at one time or another lived at the Aryan Nations compound in Hayden Lake. And with each spectacular crime The Order committed, north Idaho was projected into the international spotlight as the center of America's neo-Nazi movement and a haven for white supremacists. There seemed to have been an unending stream of news stories about The Order: their $3.6 million armored car heist in Ukiah, California the past July; armed robberies of discount stores and banks around the west that netted The Order another $2 million; the June murder in Denver of Jewish talkshow host, Alan Berg; the formal declaration of war by The Order on the "Zionist Occupation US Government"; and the electrifying, headline-grabbing shoot-outs with police in Arkansas, Alabama, Washington, Idaho, Oregon and other places that left several members of The Order either wounded or dead, as well as taking the lives of a number of law enforcement officers. All of this had a devastating affect on north Idaho's real estate business, and commerce in general. Houses were not selling and tourism was drying up.

All these crimes, Mend thought, despite Richard Butler's apparent policy of not causing trouble in the Coeur d'Alene area. The white supremacist leader's resolution to lay low locally played well with the media; they decided against spending so much time covering the Hayden Lake white supremacist group. The Aryans, at least locally, had become less newsworthy, especially after Butler resolutely disavowed any connection with The Order.

For its part, the press seemed unwilling to accept the idea that the Aryans were continuing to gain strength in north Idaho. That there had been little hate-related activity in Kootenai County was apparently enough for the media to assume the Aryan Nations was a shrinking and discredited reality.

This lull of Aryan activity in north Idaho, along with the Gilbert conviction and the passage of the Malicious Harassment law, also served to mollify the community. The Task Force on Human Relations had become inactive eighteen months earlier, once the state legislature acted on the Malicious Harassment law, and after Dina Tanners and Rick Morse left the area.

This community apathy deeply concerned Marshall Mend. He felt certain the press and the community were making the same mistake others before them had made, thinking Nazis would go away because a community was silent. Mend instinctively knew it was only a matter of time before the Aryans turned up the level of hate and violence in the Coeur d'Alene area. Nazis were like that; sooner or later their need to be in control would come into play and they would make their move.

Mend also understood something had to be done to change the public's perception about north Idaho. Fast. Whatever temporary negative publicity might result by once again bringing the Aryan Nations to the forefront of the local media would be worth it; Butler and his Nazi thugs had to be exposed for what they were. The past few months proved that keeping quiet was not going to make the problem go away. Nor would it improve national and international perceptions about north Idaho. The way you killed a rattlesnake, Mend knew, was to go after its head, even though the tail was making the most noise and attracting the most attention.

But how to do it? How could Coeur d'Alene regain its reputation as a beautiful place to vacation and a fine place to raise one's family? The first and most obvious place to begin, Mend thought, was to reactivate the Task Force on Human Relations. The Task Force had brought the community together before, and it could do it again. It could do even more than that. If managed right, the Task Force could go beyond being simply a human rights organization. It could evolve into a group that would send a steady stream of positive messages out to the world via the media to counteract the negative publicity being generated by the Aryan Nations. All the Task Force needed was the right leader.

But who could take over the helm of the Task Force now that Rick Morse had left town? Who in the community possessed the integrity, respect, organizational abilities, and public speaking skills? Who was able to bring the disparate factions of the community together? Who possessed the sensitivity and commitment to human rights and civil rights issues? Marshall Mend understood that for the Task Force to work the way he envisioned it working—to inspire the community into speaking with one voice against the Aryan Nations— it had to be representative of every political, religious, business, labor and academic group in the area.

The selection of a new Task Force leader was on his mind as he pushed out of his chair, and left his office. Newspaper under his arm he walked three doors over to the Chamber of Commerce's wood and glass office. He moved past the receptionist's desk and knocked on the door marked, "Director."

"Hi, Sandy," Mend said.

"C'mon in, Marshall," Sandy Emerson greeted.

Marshall Mend took the chair across from Emerson, dropping the newspaper on top of the business letters and other papers stacked on the desktop.

"Did you see this?" Mend asked.

"Wild, huh?"

"Yeah, wild," Mend mimicked. "Sandy, we're going to have to reactivate the Task Force."

"Why's that?"

"*Why's that?*" Mend ran his powerful hand over his forehead. He let out a long breath, "Let me ask you, before all the publicity about the Aryan Nations, The Order, and Keith Gilbert, how many inquiries did you get from families thinking about moving into the area?"

Emerson looked up at the ceiling, as if the answer to Mend's question was written on the acoustic tiles. "A guess, probably a dozen a month."

"And how many inquiries did you get from businesses that were considering relocating to north Idaho?"

Again Emerson looked up. "Six or eight a month. Again, a guess."

"How many inquiries have you averaged over the past six months?" Mend asked.

"Maybe one family a month."

"Businesses?"

Emerson's playful, questioning expression turned darkly serious. "Come to think of it, in the past six months I don't believe I've heard from more than two businesses interested in locating here."

"Exactly my point," Mend upheld, frustration and fatigue invading his normally optimistic, happy face.

"I haven't sold a house in two months," Mend added. "But I've taken a bunch of listings. People are moving out of the area and hardly anyone is moving in. For sure no blacks or Jews are wanting to settle in north Idaho. People are scared for their safety, Sandy. They'd rather live somewhere else, where they can have some peace of mind and raise their families in safety.

"Try to imagine how many companies wishing to build branch offices in the northwest don't even contact us because of the perceived racial attitudes of this area. Try to estimate how many job we've lost without even knowing it. We've got to somehow start projecting a better image of north Idaho in the media."

Emerson made a steeple with his fingers, and rested his chin on his fingertips. He fixed his pale gray eyes on Mend.

"Beyond that," Mend continued, "we'd best be ready to respond as a community when the Aryans start up again around here."

"Don't you believe the Malicious Harassment Law will make them think twice about doing anything to anyone around here?"

"Sandy," Mend scolded, as if Emerson should know, "Butler and his thugs don't give a damn about laws. They have sworn to locate the headquarters of their all-white homeland in north Idaho, which in itself is enough to drive minorities out of the area and keep others from coming in. The Aryan Nations literature is clear about its plans for Jews and people of color who are caught in the 'Aryan homeland.' Does that sound like an organization whose credo is live and let live? Like a group of people that intends to obey a law, *any* law of a government they despise and are sworn to overthrow?"

"Where do we go from here?" Emerson asked, a sense of urgency seeping into his voice.

"We need to reactivate the Task Force."

"I agree," Emerson said.

"We need someone who can both lead the Task Force and serve as its spokesperson in the community."

"Who could handle the job?"

"You mean who'd *want* the job?" Mend posed, his grin spreading across his face like butter in a warm skillet. "It has to be someone respected by all segments of the community, someone with excellent organizational skills, lots of courage, and probably not much good sense. It also has to be someone who is articulate, who can handle public speaking engagements. This person is going to be responsible for getting the word out that north Idaho is a good place to live, regardless of your color or religious preference; who can convince the world this isn't some damned Nazi homeland."

Once again Sandy Emerson looked up to the acoustic ceiling tiles for his answer. He ran his fingertips over the stubble on his chin. After a moment, he lowered his gaze, looked Marshall Mend dead in the eyes, and said, "Father Bill Wassmuth."

Mend threw his head back and laughed the loud, rumbling laugh which, along with the blue Chrysler limousine in which he chauffeured clients around town, was his trademark.

"Bill Wassmuth is the exact person I came up with," Mend agreed.

"You figure he'll take the job?"

"I don't know, but we have nothing to lose by asking.

"He's articulate. Everybody likes him. Call him and find out if he can see us."

Emerson looked up St. Pius X Church in the phone book, and dialed the number. Getting Father Bill Wassmuth on the line, he set an appointment for fifteen minutes from then.

"Let's go," Mend said as Emerson hung up the phone.

The two men hustled out of the Chamber of Commerce offices, and climbed into Mend's luxury car. They drove two miles to the north end of Coeur d'Alene, to St. Pius X Church at the top of

Haycraft Avenue.

Mend eased his car to a stop in the asphalt parking lot next to the church. The realtor paused a moment and studied the church. The spinnaker-like raked roof, and the way the earth in front of the church was graded and landscaped so the grass tapered up from the sidewalk to the corners of the raked roof, reminded Mend more of a Synagogue than a Catholic Church.

Marshall Mend and Sandy Emerson climbed out of the vehicle and walked along the sidewalk in front of the church, past the cluster of young aspens. They entered the main door located at the intersection of the church sanctuary and the religious education offices. The heels of their shoes made respectfully-quiet scuffing noises against the well-polished vinyl tile floor as they walked across the rear of the brick, wood and native rock sanctuary. The focal point of the sanctuary was a simple altar, located equidistant between two wooden sidewalls which swept upward to create a lightwell. Mounted on the front wall on each side of the altar were two brightly colored banners. Mend thought the sanctuary reminded him of what he knew about Father Bill Wassmuth: simple, lean and without frills.

Mend and Emerson moved behind the back row of pews, through the reception hall adjacent to the sanctuary, to a set of doors opening into the office area. The two men stepped into the office. Seated at the reception desk was a petite, middle-aged woman with brown shoulder-length hair held off her ears by tortoise-shell clips.

"We're here to see Father Bill Wassmuth," Mend announced.

"Go right in; he's expecting you," the woman said, her hazel eyes sparkling behind her plastic-rimmed glasses.

Mend and Emerson stepped into a medium-sized, well-lit office cluttered with books, magazines, and papers of all sizes and colors. Standing off to one side of the office was a woman in a blue skirt and white blouse. Her serious face was framed by short brown hair turning gray, and behind her glasses were eyes the color of a forest on a misty day, eyes that seemed to Marshall Mend to exude compassion.

Mend noted the name spelled out on the blue and white nameplate pinned to her blouse: Carol Ann Wassmuth.

The woman correctly read his gaze and, through a coy smile, said, "No, I'm not his wife. The church has gotten more liberal, yes, but priests still aren't able to marry."

Marshall Mend smiled sheepishly.

"I'm Bill's sister," she added, enjoying this. "I'm a Benedictine sister."

"I see," Mend added.

Carol Wassmuth stepped quietly out of the office, leaving Mend and Emerson alone with her brother.

"Hi, Father Bill," Emerson greeted, stepping across the room to shake the priest's hand.

"Sandy," Wassmuth answered. He moved to meet Emerson with the easy, light grace of an athlete.

"You know Marshall Mend?" Emerson added.

"We've met a couple of times, I think," the priest answered, and shook Mend's hand.

Mend thought the tall, lean Bill Wassmuth looked more like a golf pro than a Roman Catholic Priest in his royal blue slacks and white pullover. Mend had passed Wassmuth often on the street, him in his limo, the priest out doing his daily three mile jog. But they never really talked.

"Please, sit down," Wassmuth suggested, and escorted his two visitors to the windowed end of his office. A pair of brown fabric wing chairs and a matching couch were clustered around a round coffee table.

Mend and Emerson sat on opposite ends of the couch. Bill Wassmuth took one of the chairs, facing the two men, one long-muscled leg crossed over the other.

Mend looked carefully around the office as if appraising the place for a quick sale. The end wall was solid windows; two walls were filled with books; and the fourth had been reserved for pictures mementos, diplomas, and posters with humorously inspirational sayings such as: WHEN ALL IS SAID AND DONE, THERE IS A LOT MORE SAID THAN DONE; LIVE SIMPLY SO OTHERS MAY SIMPLY LIVE; and THINGS TO DO TODAY: 1. STOP NUCLEAR WAR 2. FLOSS.

This is not a guy who says read my lips, Mend thought. Wassmuth tells people to read his wall.

"What can I do for you?" Wassmuth asked.

"We want to reactivate the Task Force," Mend said. His attention was continually drawn to Wassmuth's marble-brown eyes. They seemed to express life's duality: sadness and joy, wisdom and naiveté, peace and anger. Deep lines crisscrossed his forehead, suggesting to Mend that no matter how protected a life the priest might have lead, Bill Wassmuth had spent time confronting his demons.

"I agree it's a good idea to get the Task Force up and moving again," the priest answered. He stroked his neatly trimmed beard, considerably darker than the frizzy blond hair on his head. "I've told several people that same thing over the past few months, ever since Dina Tanners dropped the Task Force material off here for me to keep when she left town. I was never comfortable that the Task Force and the media laid off the Aryans."

"Makes two of us," Mend clarified, excited that Wassmuth was of like mind. "All we need is to find a leader to get things rolling again."

"What about Larry Broadbent?" Wassmuth asked. "He'd be terrific."

"It has always been our view that the Task Force be headed by someone outside government or law enforcement," Mend explained. He leaned forward on the couch, his barrel chest causing the buttons of his white shirt to strain the fabric. "That way the Task Force is independent to criticize the actions of government or law enforcement, if necessary."

"Makes sense," Wassmuth acknowledged.

"We've come to ask you to take over the Task Force," Sandy Emerson interjected.

"*Me*!?" a flabbergasted Wassmuth blurted.

"You have all the qualifications," Mend put in.

"*What* qualifications do I have to lead a Human Rights organization?" Wassmuth smiled, showing white teeth that would have been perfect except the two front uppers overlapped slightly.

"About the only people of color I ever saw growing up in Greencreek, Idaho was during the summer when the wheat farmers got tanned from riding their tractors."

Sandy Emerson laughed.

"Look at it this way. The Aryans tried to intimidate Rick Morse by harassing his wife and kids," Mend picked up, his eyes sparkling. "You're not married and you don't have any kids, so you won't have to worry about your family being harassed by the Aryans. Or, worse, your wife becoming a widow and your kids orphans."

"Great," Wassmuth said, sarcastically.

"And your church is mainly brick, so they can't burn it down," Mend added.

"You say you're in sales?" Wassmuth kidded.

"You're perfect for the job," Mend finished, and cut loose with his booming laugh.

"Plus, you got one other qualification, Father Bill," Mend added. "You've got guts. You won't be intimidated by those Aryan Nazis."

Sandy Emerson drew a long breath, and held it, waiting for Wassmuth's answer.

"How do you know I have that kind of courage?" Wassmuth queried.

"I know," Mend countered.

Wassmuth slowly shook his head, then trained his eyes on the window.

"What do you say, Father Bill?" Mend posed, with the purposeful determination he used to close a sale.

His expression turning deadly serious, Wassmuth said, "I'll take the job on one condition."

"What's that?" an visibly anxious Marshall Mend asked.

"I'll only take the job if you quit calling me Father," Wassmuth said, a warm, gentle smile playing on his lips. "Just plain Bill will do. I'm nobody's father. Priests can't marry and have kids, remember?"

"It's a deal... Bill," Mend agreed, and pumped Wassmuth's hand.

Leaning back against the couch, Mend felt sated, as if he had just finished a good meal, or closed a lucrative real estate deal. He knew in his bones that the priest could turn things around for the community. And Mend realized something had to happen soon or he would be back in Los Angeles wholesaling meat.

SIXTEEN

Driving to his first meeting as Chairman of the Kootenai County Task Force on Human Relations, Bill Wassmuth found himself wondering what in his personality prompted him to become chairman or director of almost every organization in which he was involved. No matter at what level he entered an organization, he somehow worked his way into a leadership position. He was student body president in high school, the seminary, and in graduate school; ten years later, while serving as director of education for the Idaho Catholic Diocese, he was selected to chair the national committee that put together the highly controversial Catechetical Directory. This landmark document contained the proclamation that social justice was an integral part of being a Christian rather than a Sunday morning feeling.

Wassmuth smiled as he recalled how the U.S. Bishops fought to change certain portions of that Catechetical Directory, the result of three years work by the national committee he chaired. That was another thing about himself he had become aware of over the years; he was possessed by some driving, unconscious need to rock the boat.

It was much the same in the six years he had been in Coeur d'Alene. Unsatisfied with simply doing his priestly role and pastoral duties, Wassmuth served in leadership positions in the YMCA, Hospice, and Cult Awareness Center, except for the first, controversial agencies.

Now he found himself chairperson of the Task Force on Human

Relations, an association that dealt with a subject he knew little about. Growing up in the all-white farming community of Greencreek, Idaho, the first blacks he ever saw were inner-city kids who had been shipped to the Job Corps facility located near his hometown. During the winter the young black boys came to the Greencreek skating rink Wassmuth's father managed. The townspeople, suspicious of anyone different, got up in arms because the black boys were fraternizing with the town's white girls (actually, the girls had pursued the black boys, but the people of Greencreek were not satisfied to let facts stand in the way of them acting on their racism). Wassmuth's father stood up to his friends and neighbors, and refused to cave into their demands to deny the black boys entrance into the skating rink. Bill admired his father for making that stand. He believed that his father, Henry, had had his faults—rigid and controlling near the top of the list—yet the man possessed some innate sense of social justice, an instinctive knowledge of what was right and wrong. Henry Wassmuth also operated under the ethic that one person could make a difference; he believed that if you wanted to make a change you "got off your butt" and got into action. Henry passed along to his children that basic sense of fairness, along with the belief that one person could effect changes in their community. Despite that legacy from his father—or maybe because of it—Bill Wassmuth had judged black students in the seminary with him as "Oreos", black on the outside and white on the inside. Wassmuth never gave much thought to what it was like for people of color in a culture dominated by whites.

He carried this naiveté with him to his first assignment in

Caldwell, the small city thirty miles from Boise that served the farming area of southwestern Idaho. Bill attempted to minister to the spiritual needs of the Hispanic migrant workers without addressing their social needs. All he wanted to do in those days was to save the world, and escort every one of God's children along their spiritual path and through the golden archway into heaven. That was in 1969. It all changed in the summer of 1970, after attending Seattle University to study for his second Masters Degree. The post-Vatican II program at Seattle University was designed to allow priests and nuns to undergo a humanist experience that would allow them to see themselves first as men and women and human beings, then as members of the clergy. The Masters Program required three summers to complete, and the experience transformed Wassmuth. Not only was he able to live out the adolescence he never allowed himself to fully experience—he entered the seminary at fourteen— but he also underwent a soul and mind expansion in terms of his own social responsibility. Bill became a social activist in search of a cause, of which he soon found there was no shortage. From that time until this, Wassmuth had squared off at more windmills than a North Sea seagull.

He had a feeling, however, that his role of chairperson of the Task Force was really going to test his mettle. This assignment went way beyond trying to educate people out of following some charismatic, corrupt leader, as he did working with Cult Awareness; he also saw this work as more important than that at the YMCA or Hospice. This time he was going up against Nazis. And from everything he had heard about the Aryan Nations, he knew they meant business; they would not hesitate to reduce the priest population of the Idaho Diocese by one.

Such were his thoughts as he eased his car to a stop next to the North Shore Hotel in downtown Coeur d'Alene. He pushed out of the car and was about to close the door behind him when he was struck by the sobering realization of how often during the day he was alone and vulnerable to an attack. Such concerns were new to him; Wassmuth was usually a fatalist about life. He smiled at himself when he gave a quick thought to purchasing a flak-jacket for his new assignment. He shook off the wave of paranoia, and started for the front door of the hotel. Bill Wassmuth was not much for knuckling under to fear.

He pulled open the door, paused in the entryway, and checked his watch. Five minutes until twelve. He wondered how many people, if any, would show up to the first general meeting of the Task Force since the human rights group was reactivated. If Marshall Mend had anything to say about it, an amused Wassmuth surmised, there would be a full house. The real estate man, rarely given to understatement, had placed an ad in the newspaper announcing today's meeting. Beyond the time and place of the gathering, the ad contained Mend's challenge that the Task Force meeting was open to anyone interested in combating the hate and prejudice existing in their community.

Wassmuth made his way along the quiet corridor. Mend waited for him outside the wooden double doors of the meeting room. The realtor's head glowed like a hundred watt light bulb.

"Father... I mean Bill," Mend exclaimed, excitedly. "Look at this crowd, will you?"

Wassmuth peeked his head into the room. Over fifty people were crowded into the meeting room. Two men carrying handheld television cameras moved through the crowd. A reporter from a Spokane paper was arranging his audio tape recorder on the podium.

"We've *never* drawn this many people before," an excited Marshall Mend exclaimed. "We couldn't draw *flies* to a meeting before Malicious Harassment passed."

Wassmuth read between the lines; the realtor was saying that the crowd was a measure of the respect Wassmuth enjoyed in the community, an assumption that embarrassed the priest.

"Let's get to it," Wassmuth said, and leaned towards the door. He felt nervous and wanted to begin.

"The size of the crowd and the media coverage is the good news," Mend cut in, catching Wassmuth's arm.

Wassmuth braced himself.

"Butler released a statement to the press," Mend picked up, his lips struggling to match his straight face. "In it he accused you of being an undercover Jew."

"Really?" The priest chuckled.

"Being a Jew is not easy. Ask Jesus."

Wassmuth shook his head. He was beginning to like this guy.

"One other thing," Mend added.

"What can be worse than being accused of being an undercover Jew?" Wassmuth kidded.

Mend's face turned genuinely serious. "Keith Gilbert is here."

"What the hell is *he* doing here?" His stomach clenched.

"Who knows?" Mend countered.

"You don't have anything to worry about, Bill," Mend assured. "He wouldn't dare try anything in front of all these people. Besides, Larry Broadbent is here."

"Here goes nothing," Wassmuth said, sarcastically, and stepped into the meeting room.

Wassmuth took the seat in the front row reserved for him. Mend stepped to the podium and spent the next few minutes reviewing the history of the Task Force, why it had been reactivated, and what its aims were. Then he introduced Wassmuth.

Though an accomplished, well-experienced public speaker, Wassmuth felt nervous as he walked up to the podium.

"I wish to thank Marshall Mend, Sandy Emerson, Larry Broadbent, and the others who had the faith in me to ask me to serve as chairperson for the Kootenai County Task Force on Human Relations. I hope my actions justify that faith.

"Over the past few weeks I have been meeting with key members of the Task Force, and together we have come up with certain strategies that I would like to present to you this afternoon.

"First, this must be a community effort. We need to work together to provide our community with a positive avenue of responding to the presence of certain hate groups, and the bad image they've given this area in the media. The Kootenai County Task Force on Human Relations must respond to this negative publicity by speaking out in a public voice about the richness of diversity of those living in our community. We must educate others about the positive changes brought about by the civil rights movement. We must publicly reaffirm the dignity and worth of every human being who resides in Kootenai County. We must oppose bigotry and work to eliminate prejudice, for injustice done to one of our citizens is an injustice done to all of us."

Wassmuth spotted Keith Gilbert seated near the back of the room. He recognized him from newspaper and television coverage of Gilbert's trial for harassing Scott Wiley. Gilbert was smiling at him in a challenging, mocking way.

"We the people of Kootenai County are not racists," Wassmuth said, feeling a bead of perspiration work its way down the small of his back. His eyes, as if possessing a mind of their own, kept returning to Gilbert. "And in no way do we support the activity of *any* group or person that espouses hatred and violence; we will oppose their hatred and violence by positively pursuing the protection of the rights and freedoms of *all* our citizens."

Gilbert, still with that challenging, mocking grin on his face, glared at Wassmuth. No one in the room, including Gilbert, had any doubt Wassmuth was referring to the Aryan Nations. Wassmuth had resolved to meet hate and prejudice head on.

"It will be our job as members of the Task Force," Wassmuth continued, "to turn our community's frustration and anger over this racism and hatred into a positive energy for the purpose of promoting the human rights of every citizen of north Idaho. It will be up to us to reverse the trend of minorities refusing to move to north Idaho, and of those who live here, leaving the area. Our voice will stand against that of Reverend Butler's call for white supremacists to relocate to our area."

Wassmuth paused and drew a deep breath. He had given enough

public talks to know that this crowd was with him. He could sense it. He could feel it.

"I believe in our community. I believe in the love and commitment of our people. I have faith that by working together we can guarantee the basic dignity of each of our citizens," he finished.

There was a stunned silence in the room. Marshall Mend finally broke it. The realtor stood, and began applauding.

"Yeah," Mend called. "That's right."

Others around Mend got to their feet and began clapping. Before long nearly everyone in the room was standing and applauding Wassmuth.

The priest nodded, politely and modestly. He waited until they stopped clapping to continue.

"It is my feeling," Wassmuth added, "that we must organize ourselves through various working groups. We can best..."

Wassmuth was interrupted by Keith Gilbert jumping to his feet, and calling out, "What about the rights of the majority? What about the rights of the white Christian citizens of this area?"

Wassmuth's stomach clenched in a mixture of anger and fear. Despite Marshall Mend's assurances that Gilbert would not try anything violent, Wassmuth still found being in the presence of an avowed white supremacist disquieting and terrifying.

"Last time I checked," Wassmuth answered, more provocatively than he wanted, "this *is* a country of majority rule and minority rights."

"*Minority rights*?" Gilbert demanded. He stepped into the aisle. It appeared as though he might move toward Wassmuth, a prospect that did not delight the priest.

"How about *our* rights? The people who made this land into something?" Gilbert continued, jabbing his thumb into his chest. "By stating publicly that you are against white people moving to north Idaho who might be active in causes which affect their race and culture, then I submit that what you are doing is dangerously close to an infringement on freedom of association, speech and assembly."

Marshall Mend pushed to his feet and turned to stare at Gilbert.

"Look," Mend called. "We are not here to question *anyone's* right to move here or live here, or have whatever belief system they want. What we are discussing here—what this Task Force is all about—is to protect the rights of the minority, and let the world know that north Idaho is not a haven for Nazis. We want to entice people of all races, color, creeds and religion to move here."

Gilbert glared back at Mend and sneered. "As a resident of Idaho, and a native son, I resent and detest your intent to bring a lot of human garbage into this state. If you want pets, go to the pound and get dogs. They fit into our white community and your mongrel and foreign children do not."

Mend's bald head turned scarlet. Mongrel was one of the terms white supremacists used to describe Jews. To the Aryan Nations, Jews were the offspring of Satan and Eve, the evil, perverted and diseased tribe cast out of Israel by the original "seven lost tribes."

"Your Task Force would fit in well in Southern California or Miami, Florida," Gilbert sneered. "For myself, I condemn your actions and will not allow my family or children to associate with any of the misfits or niggers that you bring here. We don't dump our garbage in your yard, so why dump yours in our state?"

The television cameras closed in on Gilbert. Wassmuth thought the floodlights caused Gilbert's face to look diabolical.

An incensed Glen Walker got to his feet. "I think that if Mr. Gilbert wants to be so disruptive, and holds ideals so different from those the Task Force seeks to uphold, then maybe he ought to leave."

A chorus of voices signifying agreement with the county prosecutor's comment followed.

"Would Mr. Walker like to make a motion to that effect?" a clearly rattled Bill Wassmuth asked. He had not been prepared for anything like this.

"I so move that Keith Gilbert be asked to leave this meeting of the Task Force," Walker responded.

"I second the motion," Marshall Mend put in, never taking his eyes off Keith Gilbert.

"Any discussion of the motion?" Wassmuth asked.

"Yeah, I have something to say," Gilbert called, his face the color of bone in the white, glaring lights. "I vehemently disagree with your right to put me out of this meeting. I am a member of this community, a member of the master race of whites, and I have a right to be here."

"Any further discussion?" Wassmuth asked.

Sandy Emerson stood. "Until there is a problem, I have no objection to having the press, or any other citizen attend these meetings."

"Thank you," Wassmuth acknowledged. He looked out over the room. "Any other discussion."

Following a few beats of silence, Wassmuth posed, "All in favor of Mr. Walker's motion."

Hands went up. Wassmuth counted by pointing his index finger. "I have fourteen yeses."

"Opposed?" he queried.

Nine hands were raised, including Emerson's and Gilbert's.

"The motion passes," Wassmuth announced. He figured the quicker he got Gilbert out, the less likelihood of a fight. "You have to leave, Mr. Gilbert."

"I protest this action as violating my right of freedom of speech," Gilbert answered. He turned on his heels and headed for the door, TV camera crews trailing.

Watching Gilbert exit, Wassmuth found himself troubled about something. Before Gilbert turned to leave, he glanced at Bill Wassmuth and smiled. The neo-Nazi seemed pleased by how things had worked out.

Matters calmed down as soon as Gilbert was out of the room.

"There were a couple more things I wanted to say," Bill Wassmuth picked up, smiling weakly, trying to relax, "...before I was interrupted."

Laughter and applause from the audience.

"Looking out across the room, I am reminded that there is one group that is not represented here, one that of course should be," Wassmuth went on. "That is the Coeur d'Alene Indian tribe. They have lived in this region longer than any of us, are one of the groups hated by the Aryan Nations, and should be represented on the Task Force. I am proposing that a delegation from this group meet with the Coeur D'Alene Indian Tribal Council and invite them to be a part of the Task Force."

Heads nodded in agreement across the room.

"Good," Wassmuth continued. "Anyone who wants to go with me to talk with the Tribal Council, see me after the meeting."

Wassmuth went on to explain how he believed that the Task Force could better achieve its goals if it were divided into working groups: Victim Support; Community Response, to stage events designed to repair the bad image the community had received because of the presence of the Aryan Nations; Education, to teach children and youth about the evils of prejudice; Legislative; and Public Affairs/Speakers bureau. Those in attendance agreed with Wassmuth's suggestions and proceeded to elect a chairperson for each working group. People from the audience then volunteered to serve in the various groups.

After the meeting broke up, an excited Marshall Mend greeted Wassmuth in the corridor. The realtor bounced up and down on the balls of his feet, socking his palm.

"We did it, Father Bill... er, sorry... Bill," Mend said, excitedly. "We took a stand in there today. We let the world know that north Idaho welcomes all people, regardless of race, religion or color."

"That's right," Wassmuth answered. Though fatigued by the previous hour and a half, he found himself infected by Mend's undaunted excitement.

"We took a stand," Mend repeated. "And it's our first step in changing the image of north Idaho. We're going to tell the world that Coeur d'Alene is for everyone."

Wassmuth nodded. He realized that he and Mend differed somewhat about this issue. Mend's interest was the community's image to the rest of the country, and how that would affect the area's economic well-being. Wassmuth, on the other hand, was more interested in the human rights angle, believing it that had to come before everything else.

"You know Tony Stewart, don't you?" Marshall Mend asked, indicating the man moving towards them.

"Sure, I do. I was on his television show once, with Rabbi Gottesman," Wassmuth said, and stuck his hand out to the oval-faced, tall man with frizzy, receding, gray-flecked blond hair.

Stewart was professor of Political Science at North Idaho College, and had been active for years in various civic projects around the area. He also hosted a weekly program on the public television channel entitled, "The North Idaho College Public Forum," that dealt with social issues.

"Hi, Father Bill," Stewart greeted, with the polite drawl of his native North Carolina. He wore yellow-tinted glasses, had round shoulders and a slight overbite, causing him to look as though he was constantly smiling.

"I hope we don't get hurt in the media because we ejected Keith Gilbert from the meeting," Stewart offered.

"How could ejecting Keith Gilbert hurt us in the media?" a surprised Marshall Mend asked.

"If there is anything I know about the Aryan Nations," Stewart answered, "it is that they know how to manipulate the media. It's my guess that Gilbert set the entire scene up. He *wanted* us to ask him to leave."

"You're giving that guy too much credit," Mend dismissed.

"You're probably right," Stewart acknowledged. "I best be leaving. See you, Marshall. You need anything from me, Father Bill, just call."

"Thanks," Wassmuth said, thinking that he wanted to speak with Stewart about addressing him as Bill and not Father.

Once Stewart was out of earshot, Wassmuth asked, "What do you know about Tony?"

"He has been involved in civil rights issues since he was a kid in North Carolina. He likes to tell the story about when he was in grammar school and wrote letters to his congressman, urging him to support civil rights. His congressman wrote Tony back and told him he couldn't support the legislation.

"He's been teaching at the college since 1970," Mend continued. "Richard Butler isn't too fond of Tony because of his stand on civil rights. Tony has been coming to the Task Force meetings almost as long as I have. He knows his way around the legislature and can help with the political process."

"Good," Wassmuth completed. "Let's get him on the Task Force's legislative committee."

Mend's description of Stewart supported what Wassmuth knew about the Political Science professor. Beyond Tony Stewart's gentleness and humble demeanor was the political acumen and courage to tackle issues head on. Wassmuth had a good feeling about the prospect of working with Stewart.

"I'll be heading out," Wassmuth said. "Thanks for everything,

Marshall."

"We'll talk," Mend finished.

Wassmuth walked down the deserted corridor, and left the building. All the way he pondered what Tony Stewart said concerning how adept the Aryans were at manipulating the media. He wondered if Stewart's hunch was right that Keith Gilbert set up the scene that led to his ejection from the meeting in order to gather favorable headlines.

* * *

Wassmuth did not have to wait long for his answer; it was all over the front page of the following morning's newspaper. True to Tony Stewart's prediction, the press seized upon the incident of the Task Force ejecting Keith Gilbert from the meeting. There was a picture showing Gilbert walking out of the meeting room, the eyes of those in attendance on him. In the article Keith Gilbert was quoted as saying that the Task Force did to him what it claimed it was trying to prevent from happening to minorities: Wassmuth and the others denied him his basic rights of freedom of speech and assembly. "What kind of country is this," Gilbert asked, "where the law could be used to suppress the rights of the white majority?" Further, it was Bill Wassmuth's perception that the reporter who wrote the story was sympathetic with Keith Gilbert's point of view.

Wassmuth turned to the editorial page, which reiterated what was implied on the front page. *Everyone* in our society, the editorial stated, was guaranteed the right of free speech and assembly, no matter how unpopular the person or distasteful the views that person espoused. The editor derided the Task Force for its action of voting to expel Keith Gilbert from their meeting. The Task Force, the editor scolded, was expected to be a model for protecting the rights of the individual and not to act like villains who persecuted someone for what he or she believed. After all, the editorial continued, members of the Aryan Nations were *also* members of the community, tax-paying citizens just like Jews, Catholics, Protestants, blacks and Hispanics.

"Damn," Wassmuth said, as he slapped the palm of his hand down on his kitchen table. "My first chance at chairing a Task Force meeting and I blew it."

The idea that he was out-finessed by Gilbert and the Aryan Nations caused the hair on the back of his neck to stand on end. Gilbert took a situation designed to work against the Aryans and their cause, and transformed it to their advantage. These people, Wassmuth acknowledged, were no dupes. No matter what he had heard to the contrary, the Aryans were not a bunch of vacuous rednecks. Like Tony Stewart tried to tell him, these white supremacists were very sophisticated when it came to manipulating the press.

Wassmuth promised himself to do better next time. Especially now that he had a little clearer idea what he was up against.

Something else troubled him, beyond Keith Gilbert out-finessing him at last night's meeting, certain questions he had pondered over since the Aryan Nations had moved to north Idaho. *Why* had Butler selected north Idaho as the Aryan Nations homeland? What about the Coeur d'Alene area attracted a group like the Aryan Nations? Was it because the region was inhabited predominantly by white Christians? Or, and this was Wassmuth's fear, was it because Richard Butler sensed among the people in north Idaho an incipient racism, an attitude that would either condone or at least look the other way from the activities of the Aryan Nations? Hadn't Wassmuth heard stories about a former sheriff, John Bender, who during the early 1970's had the unspoken reputation for escorting blacks and Hispanics out of Kootenai County with the admonishment that they were not welcome there? (Done, of course, with the knowledge and tacit approval of at least some of the area's residents.) Hadn't Wassmuth been told by those who had lived in north Idaho longer than he had that as recent as seven years earlier prominent black musicians were refused entrance to area hotels and restaurants?

That his beloved north Idaho might have a deep undercurrent of racism was very troubling to Bill Wassmuth.

SEVENTEEN

Marshall Mend stopped by his office at 7:45 in the morning to pick up papers for the title company. He was alone in the office; the others would not begin arriving for an hour or so.

Mend searched through the files in his desk drawer and found the documents he needed. Before leaving he decided to make a pot of coffee so it'd be waiting for the others when they arrived. He liked his colleagues at the real estate company and enjoyed doing things for them.

While preparing the coffee maker, Mend glanced out the rear window of his office suite, located at the corner of Sherman and First in downtown Coeur d'Alene. He had a magnificent view of the park and marina, and beyond that the lake whose water was the color of hammered steel. At that moment, Mend felt right with himself and with the world.

He loved the real estate business, liked being his own boss and was good at what he did. He was better than good. Marshall Mend sold more property than any other real estate agent in Coeur d'Alene for four out of the past five years.

The coffee was dripping into the pot when the phone rang. He hustled over and answered it on the second ring, before the service picked up.

"Better Homes Real Estate," he said, politely. "Marshall Mend speaking."

"We're going to kill you one of these days, you mongrel Jew

bastard," the raspy male voice said. "The day is coming when all you Jewslime will be exterminated from this white Christian homeland."

"You lousy coward," a furious Mend countered. "Why don't you try to say that to my face, man to man."

The man on the other end of the line chuckled rheumily.

"You're no man," the caller said. "You're a Jew."

"Go to hell," Mend said.

"Just look over your shoulder. We're watching you, Jewswine. Soon it will be Yahweh to you and all the race traitors on that mongrel-loving Task Farce."

The man hung up.

Mend figured the caller knew he was alone in the office at a time when he usually was not there. He quickly glanced out the window, but did not see anything out of the ordinary. A woman walked slowl across the park towards the lake, a few people were out on the dock, tending to their boats, a boy threw a stick to a black Lab.

Mend turned back to the phone and dialed a number he knew by heart.

"Kootenai County Sheriff's Department," sounded the woman's voice.

"Larry Broadbent there?" Mend was acting on Broadbent's instructions to report immediately any incidents of threats or harassment.

"I'm sorry but Undersheriff Broadbent isn't in his office. Shall I try to reach him on the radio?"

"Just tell him Marshall Mend called."

"Your number?"

"He has it. Thank you."

Mend hung up, jammed the legal papers he needed for the title company into his jacket pocket, and walked outside. He crossed the parking lot, pausing next to his car. The realtor looked quickly in both directions before turning to his car. Instead of opening the car door, Mend lowered himself to one knee and checked the undercarriage for anything suspicious. He straightened, walked to the front of the car and lifted the hood. Once satisfied a bomb had not been installed on his car, he closed the hood, walked around to the driver's side, and sat down behind the wheel. Despite his precautions, Mend felt a flutter of fear when he turned the ignition key. The engine caught and he shifted into gear.

"What a way to live," he said to himself. He pulled out of the parking lot on to Sherman Street, his earlier feeling of serenity all but a memory.

Mend decided to stop for breakfast before going by the title company. He drove out to Perkins, the coffee and pancake restaurant located on Government Way, near the Interstate. He bought a paper out of the machine, took a spot at the counter, and ordered coffee from the waitress.

He was well into his first refill of coffee, and absorbed in an article about a new motel proposed for the area near Perkins Restaurant, when four beefy men wearing camouflage clothing and green berets sauntered up to a nearby table and sat down.

Initially Mend was afraid they might be looking for him, though quickly realized his fear was unwarranted. Taking someone out in a public place was not the Aryans' style. They tended to do things on the sly; they bombed your house or caught you alone to do their dirty work. His initial feeling of dread past, Mend experienced what he could best describe as a primitive, psychic fear, almost a genetic thing that came naturally to those like him who were members of the most persecuted race in history. Marshall Mend's Jewish blood was speaking to him.

Mend turned back to his newspaper and took a sip of coffee. However, he was unable to concentrate on the newspaper or enjoy his coffee. The quartet of neo-Nazis sitting a few feet away from him in the restaurant caused images to move through his head like a grainy black and white home movie.

First he saw his daughter's drawn look when she told him she had received menacing phone calls over the past several months. The caller stated she was a mongrel Jewess and threatened her with death. Mend's initial reaction was anger with his daughter for not telling him about the calls sooner. He quickly backed off, recognizing he was turning some of the anger and frustration he felt for the Aryans towards his daughter. She did not deserve that. She was scared to death, the poor kid. Fifteen years old, and she had to endure that brand of hatred. After she told him about the calls, Mend alerted Larry Broadbent, who arranged to have a tap put on the realtor's phone. The calls kept coming, but whoever was making them was smart; they called from pay phones, did not stay on long enough for the call to be traced, and never used the same phone twice.

Then there was his wife, Dolly. So much had changed for her since they had moved to Coeur d'Alene. Initially she was extremely happy to have left Los Angeles and all the problems that went along with big city living. She saw north Idaho as the ideal place to raise her daughter. For the first time in her life she felt comfortable leaving her car unlocked when she went into a store. She even stopped bolting the door of her house during the day. But all that changed once the Aryan Nations became a force in the area. She confided in Marshall that she never would have consented to move to Idaho if she had known the neo-Nazis were located here. She had become a nervous wreck. She was afraid for her life, as well as for the lives of her husband and daughter. She insisted that Marshall buy her a dog to protect her while her husband was at work and her daughter was in school. She convinced Marshall—although he did not need much coaxing—to install a silent alarm device on their house. Further, this once independent, friendly woman became afraid to leave her house alone. Her husband accompanied her almost everywhere, including to the supermarket.

Then there were the threatening calls, like the one this morning, Marshall Mend had received over the past year or so, calls that became more frequent the past couple of months. They came at various hours of the day and night to both his home and office. It was never the same person, but the messages were similar: "We're watching you Jewswine. Soon it will be Yahweh to you and all the race traitors on that Task Farce." It was as if each caller read from the same cue card, which would not have surprised Mend, as he did not think any of the Aryans had enough brains to speak spontaneously. If any of them possessed more than a shoe size-IQ, Mend figured, they never would have fallen for Butler's hate rhetoric in the first place.

Probably the most frightening, eerie incident occurred the previous week. He stopped by a downtown photo shop managed by a friend. The photo shop manager asked Marshall if he was selling his house. A puzzled Mend said no, and asked why his friend thought he was. The friend reported that he noticed some pictures of Mend's house in a roll of film he had recently processed. The manager of the photo store showed Mend the pictures. Marshall nearly became sick to his stomach looking at them. His house had been photographed from almost every conceivable angle, as if whomever snapped off the pictures was putting together a file for inspection by a bank appraiser. Or, Mend thought grimly, someone was casing his house. The film was dropped off by a man from Hayden Lake, a name Mend did not recognize. Upon checking later with Larry Broadbent, Mend learned that whoever left the roll of film to be processed either used an alias or did not reside in Hayden Lake.

Then there was the incident that occurred earlier in the month at the St. Pius X parish festival. Marshall Mend had volunteered to pull a stint in the dunk tank, the proceeds of which, along with those of the other booths at the parish festival, went to benefit the church fund. Mend's job was to perch on a metal seat while various people bought chances to throw a softball at a metal disk located above his head. If the person hit the disk, a spring-loaded rod running to Mend's seat was activated, the seat released, and the real estate man dropped into the tank of water. In ten minutes on the perch, no one, including Bill Wassmuth—who had tried twice—hit the bull's eye. It was a fun thing, Mend taunting people he knew to take their chances, and these same friends attempting to put him in the water. Mend's mood changed quickly, however, when a man wearing a white power T-shirt, camouflage pants and matching hat purchased tickets for the dunk tank. He recognized the man as Ed Hawley, a resident of the Aryan Nations compound at Hayden Lake, and one of Butler's personal bodyguards. Mend's face turned ashen, and he climbed quickly down out of the dunk tank. Mend hustled over to the other side of the festival grounds and alerted Bill Wassmuth. Hawley, however, left before they could return to the dunk tank.

Yeah, Mend thought as he sipped his coffee at the counter of Perkins Restaurant, the past few months had been especially trying on him and his family. He also understood that these past months had changed him in a way he did not like. Normally a carefree man given to humor and fun, he had turned more careful and driven. That he and his family were singled out by the Aryans caused him to feel angry and persecuted. At times he seriously entertained the idea of selling everything for which he had worked over the past five years, and getting the hell out of north Idaho. That was only a fleeting thought, however. He knew he would never cut and run. He was not built that way; he had been a fighter all his life. Besides, he understood that if he ran, the Aryans won. One more member of the area's ever-decreasing minority population gone, and the neo-Nazis that much closer to their dream of an all white homeland. Thank God for the Task Force, Marshall Mend thought. He may have felt frustrated, angry and persecuted over the past few months, but due to the encouragement and support from members of the Task Force he had never felt isolated. Wassmuth, Tony Stewart, Larry Broadbent and the others had been enormously supportive of him and his family, and of their right to live anywhere they chose. Mend suspected that if it was not for the Task Force, the fear he suffered for his and his family's welfare might have gotten to him and he might have moved out of the area.

There was another reason Marshall Mend hung in and stood up the Aryan Nations. He believed in what the Task Force was trying t do. Mend understood instinctively that the Task Force's program of education—especially the impassioned and eloquent talks given throughout north Idaho and eastern Washington by the tireless Bill Wassmuth about the danger posed to any community by hate groups and the inspiration the priest offered to each of those communities about the need to continually affirm the rights of all their citizens— was taking its toll on the Aryans. The influence Richard Butler and the other Aryans exerted over members of the north Idaho communi was waning. And, Mend believed, finally a balance was developing between the coverage the media accorded to the sensational, headline-grabbing activities of the Aryans and that given to the Tasl Force's seminars and events. North Idaho was beginning to be portrayed in newspapers and on television as a place where hate groups of any kind were unwelcome. Certain Task Force events suc as the Martin Luther King Day celebration—held at North Idaho College and drawing over 1000 people—were covered widely on television and radio and in the area's major newspapers.

There was another barometer Marshall Mend used to measure tl turnaround in north Idaho, the indicator he trusted most of all: his real estate business had picked up considerably in the last year or sc Once again he was selling houses to new families moving into the community. And the listings he was taking for houses to sell were mostly from people moving across town, or from those leaving the area because of a company transfer or some other reason not related to the Aryans. The flight from Coeur d'Alene and the surrounding areas had slowed to a trickle. All indicators pointed to a resurgence of the population growth of the 1970's and a return of the tourist trade.

Mend had become a believer of Bill Wassmuth's philosophy that nonviolence, education and a strategy of responding positively to hate was paying off.

The beeper on Mend's belt sounded, jolting him from his thoughts. He checked the number. He dropped a dollar on the counter, folded the newspaper and jammed it under his arm, and pushed from the stool. Turning to leave, he was taken by a chill, as if someone opened a window in the middle of the winter. One of the Aryans sitting at the nearby table watched him with a baleful glare. Mend did his best to ignore him. The realtor walked determinedly across the dining room. He stopped by the door and dropped a quarter into the pay phone. He dialed, and waited for an answer.

"This is Marshall Mend," he said to the woman who answered.

"Yes, Mr. Mend," she responded, eagerly. "Larry Broadbent wants to talk with you...Hang on, I'll patch you through."

Waiting for Broadbent, Mend turned to face the Aryans. He did not like neo-Nazis at his back.

Larry Broadbent's voice came through what sounded like a snowstorm.

"Marshall," Broadbent said, with a sense of uncommon urgency.

"What are you doing?"

"On my way to my office. Why?"

"Can I see you for a couple of minutes?" Broadbent asked, his voice cut off by the hissing sound.

"Sure. Where?"

"Meet me up on Lookout Drive, by the sharp turn."

"I'm on my way." Marshall Mend felt a sense of panic as he hung up the phone.

His mind raced as he left the restaurant. Broadbent wanted to meet him just a few blocks from the realtor's house. Mend wished to hell he would have had the presence of mind to ask the cop what this was all about. He hated this kind of suspense.

Once in the parking lot he checked around to be certain no one was watching him. He casually lowered himself to one knee, and checked the undercarriage of his car. Then he lifted the hood.

It took Mend about five minutes to reach the classy residential area along Loch Haven Drive. Broadbent waited for him alongside the road, leaning against his unmarked car.

The realtor eased his Chrysler to a stop in back of Broadbent's car. He opened the door and stepped out.

"What's going on, Larry?" Mend greeted, trying to appear casual. The worried look on Broadbent's face further spiked his anxiety level.

Broadbent turned his eyes towards the concrete retaining wall that held the adjacent wooded hill off the roadway. Painted in large white letters along almost the entire length of the retaining wall were the words, KILL MARSHALL MEND. Next to Mend's name was large swastika.

Marshall Mend's head turned scarlet. "Those lousy Nazis," he hissed through gritted teeth.

Mend stormed back to his car. He threw open the trunk and pulled out the can of white spray paint he used to touch up his real estate signs. He tore off his jacket and tossed it on top of the hood of his car. Rolling up the sleeves of his white shirt as he walked, he moved to a spot in front of the retaining wall.

"Hold on a second," Larry Broadbent called. "We need to get a picture of the writing before you paint it out."

"There's a Polaroid camera on the front seat of my car," Mend revealed. He seemed unable to take his eyes off the writing, as if he could somehow stare away its implications.

Broadbent stepped alongside him. The Undersheriff pointed the camera at the wall and clicked off a photo. He waited for the camera to spit out the exposed photo, then took another to make certain. Broadbent held the photos out in front of him, and watched as they transformed from charcoal brown, to sepia, to a picture of the writing on the wall.

"Got it," Broadbent said.

Marshall Mend fell to the task of painting out the words and the swastika. He was halfway through the job when Broadbent touched his arm.

"Let me help."

All the fury and fear and frustration of the past couple of years boiled up within Marshall Mend at that instant. As sometimes happened with him, he turned it on someone who did not deserve it, someone who just happened to be in the way.

"What the hell do you know about any of this?" Mend snapped. "I'm the one those stinking Nazis are after. I'm the Jew, remember? This is my fight. You're getting paid to do what you do. You go home at five o'clock and forget the hate. I get to live with it, twenty-four hours a day. I get to watch my family get a little crazier each day from the shame and anger and fear they feel because there are people who believe we don't even have a right to exist, just because I happen to be Jewish. Can you imagine that, Larry? Do you have any idea what it's like to feel as though you don't belong on this planet because of who you are?"

Broadbent did not flinch or otherwise show any outward emotion.

"For the record," Larry Broadbent said, softly, gently, "you're not the only Task Force Member they're going after. Ginny DeLong receives a crank call late at night after every Task Force meeting, to let her know they know where she's been. Skip Kuck had a brick thrown through her front window a couple of months ago. Norm Gissel gets threatening phone calls. You know Norm's wife is Palestinian? The crank caller accuses Norm and his wife and children of being mongrels and children of Satan."

Marshall Mend stopped painting and turned to Broadbent. Much of the anger ebbed from him, as if Broadbent's words lanced a boil deep within him.

"That it?" Mend asked, quietly, feeling a little foolish and selfish. He took a few deep breaths to calm himself; he had not done much breathing the last few minutes. "How about you, Larry? They been hassling you?"

Broadbent smiled. "I'm a cop. Threats on my life are part of the cost of doing business."

"Lowlifes," Mend picked up. "What have they been doing?"

Broadbent's features softened.

"Phone calls and letters, mostly," he explained. "They say I'm a traitor to my race, a nigger- and Jew-lover, and marked for death."

Mend shook his head.

Broadbent's lips formed into a small smile. "I wouldn't care if it was just me... Shoot, I'd like to have a hundred bucks for every death threat I've received since I've been a cop. This bunch has threatened to blow up my house and kill my family. People like that ought to leave a man's family out of it."

"I'm sorry you have to go through this."

Broadbent waved him off.

"Like I said a minute ago," Mend continued, his eyes taking on a warm sparkle, "at some level it really isn't your fight."

Broadbent's gray/green eyes turned hard, and his face went white. It was the first time Mend ever saw Broadbent angry.

"Look," Broadbent said, firmly, "when you or any citizen is threatened, it's my fight. Someone like you gets hurt because of your religion, then we all get hurt. Today it's you because you're a Jew, tomorrow it's me because I'm a cop, or a Mason, or a Dodger fan. These Nazis won't be satisfied until they pick us all off, one at a time."

Mend smiled. "I didn't know you were a Dodger fan. No wonder I liked you right from the start."

A small, almost apologetic smile appeared on Broadbent's lips.

Mend thought there was something about Broadbent that summed up the solidarity and support the realtor felt over the past months from the members of the Task Force. It touched Marshall Mend deeply.

"So," Broadbent asked, pointing at the wall, "can I help paint this garbage out, or not?"

Mend handed Broadbent the spray can.

Mend watched Larry Broadbent finish painting out the swastika. Marshall felt a great kinship for the burly, quiet Undersheriff. He did not feel quite so imperiled knowing a guy like Larry Broadbent was standing up for his rights. Though not much given to things esoteric, Mend thought there was something symbolic about the act of Broadbent, a Christian, painting out the swastika.

Once finished, Broadbent put the cap back on the can, and reached down for a handful of grass to clean his fingers. He turned to Mend. "You okay?"

"Yeah, I'm okay," Marshall answered. "I'd just like to see those Nazis the hell out of here. Out of this state, out of this country."

The twinkle returned to Broadbent's eyes. "Not sure the Task Force can go that far... Maybe the best we can hope for is to continue what we're doing, and maybe the Aryans will choke in their own hate."

"You mean like Napoleon said." Mend took the can of paint from Broadbent. "'Never interfere with your enemy when he's in the process of destroying himself.'"

Broadbent smiled. "Something like that, yeah."

"Let's get the hell out of here," Mend suggested.

EIGHTEEN

Seattle

John Goldmark settled into the tan barrel-shaped rocker situated in front of the big bay window that looked out over Puget Sound. It was raining, the water streaking the window made the lights across the Sound look psychedelic. The Bainbridge Island Ferry was barely visible through the mist.

An attorney, Goldmark was glad to be off freeways crowded with people dashing between shopping malls to complete last minute shopping, and out of the way of those emerging tanked-up from Christmas Eve office parties. A Jew, tonight was not his night; he was satisfied to spend it safe and dry and quiet with his wife and two young children.

The tall, dark-haired, lean man reached down alongside the chair, into the brass magazine holder for the book he was reading. He opened the hardcover, rubbed the bottoms of his stocking feet against the carpet, and began reading.

Goldmark became so absorbed in his book he did not see the figure move past the window in the dark. Nor did he hear the laundry room window slide open a few seconds later. The laundry room, next to the garage, was a good forty feet and three rooms from where Goldmark sat reading. The only sounds he was aware of were the windblown bushes rubbing against the side of his house, and the muted gabble of the television upstairs in his children's room. There was no school the following day, so his son and daughter were not restricted on the amount of television they were allowed to watch. Goldmark's wife was also upstairs, taking a bath.

Goldmark never heard David Lewis Rice, the white supremacist Duck Club member, walk up behind him. (The Duck Club was one of the many loosely knit white supremacist organizations that supported Richard Butler and his Aryan Nations.) He saw Rice's reflection in the window before he heard him, and, at the same instant, the startled attorney turned and came halfway out of his chair. He paused when he realized that the slight, short man with the curly brown hair had an automatic pistol trained on him.

"What the hell?" Goldmark uttered.

"Sit back down, you Commie kike bastard," Rice ordered.

A stunned and panic-stricken John Goldmark did as he was told.

"Commie? I'm not a Commun," Goldmark protested.

He never got the chance to finish his statement. The silencer-equipped automatic pistol made a noise like a hoarse cough, and the bullet caught Goldmark in the throat, passing through his neck and severing his spinal column. John Goldmark was dead before he slumped back against his favorite chair.

"Yahweh to you," Rice said, without feeling. "Yahweh to a member of the Commie kike Jewocracy."

David Lewis Rice turned and tiptoed quietly upstairs. His automatic pistol coughed four more times, then the house fell silent again. The next sound was the quick, stabbing scream of a woman. The gun coughed twice more, quieting the scream.

David Lewis Rice walked back downstairs. He paused to slip his gun into the pouch-pocket of his camouflage-style pants. He left the house by the front door.

The Goldmark house was silent, except for the rasping sound of bushes scraping the side of the house and the muted gabble of the television.

NINETEEN

"Sure hope they go for it, Marshall," Norm Gissel said from the back seat of Mend's car.

Seated next to Norm Gissel, Coeur d'Alene attorney and Task Force member, was Bill Wassmuth. In the passenger seat was Skip Kuck, another Task Force member. Kuck, who wore her gray-dusted brown hair short, had a round gentle face. She joined the Task Force after being appalled by the racially based incidents going on around Coeur d'Alene. Kuck, with Gissel, Mend and Wassmuth, were on their way to the Coeur d'Alene Indian Tribal Council Headquarters.

"Makes two of us," Mend answered, keeping his eyes on the road.

"It's going to be dicey," Gissel suggested.

The baby-faced attorney wore his straight brown hair combed to one side. He had sympathetic brown eyes behind plastic-rimmed glasses, and a mischievous, ready smile. Raised in the southern Idaho town of Payette—the same town in which baseball great Harmon Killebrew grew up—Gissel had been moved towards intellectual openness by his education. He became interested in the civil rights movement in law school, but had not become an activist until he lived for a time in the South. While in Mississippi, he was appalled at how blacks were treated, and felt moral indignation at the separate amenities for whites and blacks. The incidents that affected Gissel the most profoundly, however, were the murder of Medgar Evers, and the tragedy in Alabama in which the Klan blew up a church, killing five people. Even at that, Norm Gissel only felt the tragic sting of racism as an observer. He moved from compassionate observer to a victim, however, when he married a Palestinian woman and moved to north Idaho, where he received threatening phone calls for being a race traitor and miscegenist.

Skip Kuck smiled as she ventured, "Don't you find it a little odd that we white folk are on our way to meet with the Coeur d'Alene Indian Tribal Council to ask them for help in protecting the rights of minorities, especially after we've spent the better part of our history trampling all over *their* rights?"

Bill Wassmuth stared out the window, mesmerized by the vast pine forest. "The past several years, beginning with Reagan, haven't helped," Wassmuth theorized. "Ronnie, George and their gang set back the civil rights movement by at least thirty years."

Marshall Mend caught Norm Gissel's eye in the rearview mirror. The two men looked at one another in a way that indicated there was something they wanted to say but were hesitant to bring up.

"I feel dishonest going out to ask these people to participate in a system that has been screwing them for the past five hundred years," Wassmuth added, with undisguised rancor. "Especially after the promise of the sixties."

Mend and Gissel once again looked at one another in the rear view mirror.

"Bill," Marshall Mend began, hesitantly, "I don't know how to say this, but I have a problem with some of your attitudes about politics."

"Me, too," Gissel piped in.

Wassmuth turned to Skip Kuck for support.

"I agree with Marshall and Norm," the woman said softly and politely. "I'm sorry, Bill."

A slightly taken aback Wassmuth turned to the two men. He could tell it was hard for them to bring this up. He smiled, to take some of the pressure off, before asking, "What are you getting at?"

"You've done an incredible job as spokesperson for the Task Force," Mend said, haltingly. "You're educating thousands of people about the value of upholding the human rights of every person. But I think your politics are starting to get in the way of the message."

"How do you mean?" Wassmuth asked.

"For the Task Force to work," Norm Gissel picked up, "it has to be a non-partisan thing. We need the help of everyone in the community: Republicans, Democrats, left-wingers, right-wingers, and middle-of-the-roaders. We can't alienate someone because he or she has different political beliefs than you or me, or Marshall, who happens to be a Republican. For that matter we have to be careful we don't alienate anyone on the Task Force."

"Am I alienating people?" Wassmuth asked incredulously.

"Afraid so," Marshall Mend reported. The skin around his eyes was taut and his lips pulled white over his teeth. "Friends of mine—conservatives like me—have mentioned they're reluctant to join the Task Force because they see it as a liberal movement."

Wassmuth's face burned with anger and embarrassment. His immediate inclination was to defend himself, to deny that he had turned this thing into a partisan issue. He had the presence of mind, however, to realize that whenever he found himself having to defend himself, thus denying the reality or perception of those around him—people like Mend, Gissel and Kuck who brought up some difficult issue—it was generally an indication he needed to hear what they had to say. The priest knew himself well enough to understand how insidiously self-righteous his ego could be.

Wassmuth took a deep breath, swallowed a couple of times, and raked his fingers through his hair.

"I didn't realize I was doing that," he answered, his initial flush of anger and defensiveness giving way to guilt. He hated to screw things up, or hurt the feelings of others. "I'm really sorry if that's what I've been doing."

"We're dead in the water if we make this a political or a partisan issue, Bill," Mend instructed, with a sly smile. "You need us conservatives. Remember, we're the ones with the money and, in this state especially, power. We're as opposed to what the Aryan Nations stands for as you are."

Wassmuth nodded his acknowledgment.

"Just stay with the human rights issue and you'll do fine," Gissel added. "The message is enough. Avoid indicting Reagan, Bush, Gingrich, the Republicans, conservatives, or anyone. They didn't invent hate. Don't even insinuate they did, by innuendo or in jest."

The four people in the car fell silent for a few moments. It was left to Wassmuth to puncture the balloon of tension that filled the car.

"I really appreciate you having the courage to say what you did," Wassmuth said. "I get carried away, sometimes."

Norm Gissel reached over and lightly massaged Wassmuth's shoulder.

"We're *all* still under construction," Gissel acknowledged warmly.

"That's for sure," Wassmuth added. His mind was busy rehashing some of the talks he had given lately for evidence of what Mend, Kuck and Gissel were talking about.

They drove another couple of miles through the pine forest in silence.

"Marshall, this is a nice car," Norm Gissel said, finally, as he ran his hand along the top of the plush leather seat.

"I love it," Mend answered. He held the black steering wheel in a straight-armed fashion like a race driver taking his car into a turn.

"The real estate business must be pretty good," Gissel added, with a smile.

"Not doing bad for a white man," Mend tossed, and matched Gissel's smile with one of his own.

Wassmuth could not believe his ears.

"Marshall," he said directly, yet politely. "What you just said— 'not bad for a white man'—is a racist comment."

Wassmuth felt warm under the collar. He did not want Mend to think he was playing get-back because Marshall and the others brought up the business about keeping the Task Force non-partisan. Plus, it was naturally difficult for Wassmuth to confront anyone, friends especially, who told a racist or ethnic joke, or uttered a racial slur.

Mend's face paled, as if his heart was on holiday. He relaxed his grip on the steering wheel and slumped in his seat. "Dang," he said.

Wassmuth braced himself. He expected Mend to attack him, or

attempt to justify his comment.

"You're right," Marshall commented. "It *was* a racist comment. I'm sorry."

Wassmuth looked at Mend with compassion and understanding. "Hey," the priest assured, "it's okay. We're all under construction, remember?

"Besides, if you feel *that* bad about it, I'm ready to hear your confession any time."

Marshall Mend chuckled. "You can overhear something as a kid, repeat it all your life, and never realize you're hurting someone each time you say it. I want you guys to call me on it whenever I say something like that, okay?"

"With pleasure," Norm Gissel kidded.

Gissel ran a hand across his silky hair as if he was straightening it. "I can relate, being raised with no exposure to blacks or other minorities. Insensitivity and ignorance are awfully close to racism."

"I identify," Wassmuth added. "I feel as though I was brought up in a hermetically sealed environment."

"Ditto," Skip Kuck agreed.

There followed another few moments of silence, the only sound the car's tires slapping against the breaks in the pavement.

"None of us had much to say about how we were raised," Norm Gissel offered, "but we sure as hell can do something about how we are now."

Mend smiled at Wassmuth in the rear view mirror.

"Leave it to a lawyer to put things in historical context, eh, Bill?" Mend kidded.

"Hope he doesn't send us a bill for his time," Wassmuth added, with a chuckle.

"Ah, you guys," Gissel finished, waving them off.

Mend piloted his car along the narrow road until he came to a small paved road that intersected the highway from the right. He took the county road and drove for a few miles, past a sawmill, to the Tribal Council Headquarters. The Council Headquarters was a modern one-story, wood and glass structure, that seemed somehow out of place against the encroaching, thick forest. Several vehicles, mostly pickup trucks, cozied up like nursing puppies to the side of the building.

"Here we are," Mend announced.

The four of them climbed from the car. Wassmuth leading the way, they ascended a set of wooden stairs and entered the building. They walked directly into a well-lit comfortably furnished reception area whose rear wall was adorned with a large weaving. The receptionist, a heavy-set, middle-aged, Native American woman, looked up at the contingent and smiled.

"We're from the Kootenai County Task Force on Human Relations," Norm Gissel announced. "We have an appointment with the Tribal Council."

"Of course," the receptionist answered. "You can go right in. They're expecting you."

Wassmuth, Gissel, Mend and Kuck stepped through a set of double doors into a spacious chamber. In the center of the room was a horseshoe-shaped table. Several men sat at one end; four vinyl-covered chrome chairs had been placed in the open end.

The man seated dead center at the end of the table was dressed in a red and yellow flannel shirt and blue jeans. His black hair clipped to his shirt collar, he watched with brooding, mournful black eyes as the Task Force contingent entered the Tribal Council chambers.

"Ernie," a slightly nervous Bill Wassmuth began, greeting Ernie Stensgar, president of the Coeur d'Alene Tribal Council.

Despite knowing Stensgar, Wassmuth felt anxious because of the importance and the setting of the meeting. He sensed the Tribal Council members were cautiously distant, something that further unnerved the priest. "We appreciate you seeing us."

"Hello, Father Bill," Stensgar greeted. "Please make yourself comfortable."

The Task Force members settled themselves into the empty chairs.

"We need your help and advice," Wassmuth started, getting right to it.

The lights in the room reflected against Ernie Stensgar's coal black eyes like campfires against the night.

"What can we do to help improve relations between our community and your tribe?" Wassmuth asked.

Stensgar nodded expectantly.

"You may have heard," Wassmuth went on, "that we've scheduled a five state human rights celebration for next month. We've come to ask that the Coeur d'Alene Tribe be a part of the celebration."

Stensgar glanced right, then left. The Council members, dressed in leather vests and bead necklaces, long hair in pony tails, sat silently.

"Who else is going to participate in your gathering?" Stensgar asked.

"I'll let my colleagues answer for their part," Wassmuth replied.

"I've sent out over 2000 letters to cities and counties all over the northwest," Norm Gissel picked up, "asking each community to issue a proclamation upholding the human rights of all citizens, and stating its opposition to hate groups. So far, over two hundred communities have written back with proclamations."

Stensgar turned down the corners of his mouth, a gesture Wassmuth interpreted as a sign he was impressed by Gissel's numbers.

"We've invited the Governors of Idaho, Oregon, Washington, Montana and Wyoming," Marshall Mend reported. "All but Wyoming have committed to sending their governor or a representative."

"Sounds good," the Tribal Council President said.

"NBC, CBS, ABC, CNN and some of the other networks will have crews there," Skip Kuck added, "along with reporters from the various newspapers, including the *New York Times*."

"Appears as though you have all the bases covered," Stensgar said. "Why do you need us?"

"The Coeur d'Alene Tribe is an important part of our community," Wassmuth picked up. "We need your participation for this thing to work."

Stensgar looked across the table at Wassmuth. His expression softened and his eyes shone. "You have an interesting sense of timing, Father Bill."

"How's that?" Wassmuth asked.

"Scheduling your Human Rights Celebration the same weekend as the Aryan Nations annual World Congress." The Tribal Council President's lips moved slowly into a smile. "Or was that just a coincidence? One of those things?"

Wassmuth felt less nervous. "We planned it that way. We wanted to show the world the positive side of north Idaho and blunt the effects of the media coverage of the Aryan Congress."

"I see," Stensgar ventured, his eyes reflecting his amusement.

"We want to show the richness of the ethnic diversity of this area," Wassmuth explained, choosing his words carefully. "And you're a big part of that richness."

Wassmuth understood all too well that if this Human Rights Celebration was going to work it was going to have to be more than an afternoon of white activists talking about how minorities were honored and welcome in north Idaho. The Task Force would look silly if there was hardly more than token attendance at the Human Rights Celebration by north Idaho's largest minority group, the Coeur d'Alene Indians.

"I'm told you did very well last fall with your symposium," Stensgar noted.

Wassmuth leaned back in his chair. The symposium, Racism: Prejudices and Progress, was held the previous September at North Idaho College. The five-day affair dealt with racism from the perspectives of Afro-Americans, Native Americans, Mexican Americans and Jewish Americans, and featured speakers such as

Civil Rights Worker and former Congressman Julian Bond, former US Ambassador to Mexico Julian Nava, Menominee (Wisconsin) Tribal Council President Ada Deer, and the Governor of Idaho. Except for attending the talk by Ada Deer, the Coeur d'Alene Tribe did not support the symposium in any great number.

"It was a beginning," Wassmuth said, diplomatically. "We want our Human Rights Celebration to be better. We'd like you to provide one of the speakers."

"And we'd like someone from the Coeur d'Alene Tribe to sit on the Board of the Task Force," Norm Gissel cut in, "and help make policy decisions about Human Rights issues in north Idaho."

Ernie Stensgar nodded thoughtfully, again checking each direction to see if any of the Tribal Council members had anything to say.

Wassmuth took a deep breath. He sensed that he and the others from the Task Force had accomplished their mission.

"Let us talk about it among ourselves," Stensgar said. "We'll get back to you."

"Of course," Wassmuth finished, pushing to his feet. "We'll look forward to hearing what you have to say."

The faces of the Tribal Council members were more animated than earlier, each man stood and warmly shook hands with the representatives of the Task Force.

A confident, happy Wassmuth led Mend and the others out of the Tribal Council offices. On the way to Mend's car, Wassmuth considered that the four of them coming out here today to ask the Coeur d'Alene Tribal Council for their help was the first time in anyone's memory that white leaders of Coeur d'Alene had extended such a gesture to the Native American Tribe.

TWENTY

The morning before the Human Rights Celebration, Bill Wassmuth was so jumpy and had consumed so much coffee he swore he was wearing out the *inside* of his clothes.

He would need all the energy he had; there were dozens of last minute details to be looked after. It was not every day that over a thousand people and a couple hundred members of the media filed into Coeur d'Alene's City Park for a day of speeches, ethnic singing, dancing and cultural displays. Keeping all that straight would have been enough. Matters were complicated, however, by the reality that a few miles from Coeur d'Alene City Park, several hundred representatives from white supremacist hate groups from all over the U.S. and Canada were gathering at the Aryan Nations compound at Hayden Lake for the sixth annual Aryan Congress. The white supremacists were due to espouse their philosophy of hate, and to discuss their plan to create an all-white homeland in the Pacific Northwest. It was well known that the Aryans were fighting-mad at Wassmuth and the Task Force for upstaging the white supremacists' Congress in the media with their Human Rights Celebration.

In addition to his responsibilities of seeing that the Human Rights Celebration came off as planned, Wassmuth had to attend to his normal parish duties. He had a wedding to perform at three o'clock that day. Which meant he had to somehow choreograph his participation in the Human Rights Celebration—including presenting the opening speech—with what was going on at St. Pius X Church.

All that would have been enough to keep Wassmuth in a state of being three steps from a nervous breakdown. However, at 7:30 that morning one more brick was added to his load with the call from Idaho Governor John Evans' aide.

"Sorry, Bill," the male aide explained. "The Governor will be held up in Sandpoint this morning, and then he has to be in Burley at four o'clock to give another speech. The State plane is propeller-driven, and there simply isn't enough time to stop through Coeur d'Alene then get him to Burley by three thirty. He won't be able to appear at your Human Rights Celebration."

"Hold it," Wassmuth said, thinking fast. "You mean the only thing standing between the Governor making it to Coeur d'Alene or not is a faster plane? A jet?"

"That's right," the aide acknowledged.

Wassmuth was in a bind. Governor Evans *had* to be here today. The governors of three other states—Washington, Oregon and Montana—had chosen to send representatives to the Human Rights Celebration rather than appear in person. That was bad enough. But Coeur d'Alene was in Idaho, and Coeur d'Alene was where the real and symbolic struggle against the Aryan Nations was taking place. Governor Evans' appearance would lend immense credibility to the Human Rights Celebration. He did not show, Evans would be sending out another message, that the issue of human rights was not high on Idaho's agenda.

"If I can get hold of a private jet," Wassmuth continued, "and fly him to Burley in time to make his speech there, would the Governor reconsider coming to our Celebration?"

"I'm sure he would. But let me check and call you back," the aide explained.

"I'll see what I can do about producing a jet," Wassmuth finished, and hung up.

He grabbed the telephone directory. Before opening it, he paused, and glanced upwards for a moment to calm himself. He said a quick prayer, then smiled at himself. He wondered if his act of trying to line up a jet to bring Governor Evans to Coeur d'Alene was an updated, high-tech version of the loaves and fishes number.

He opened the telephone book to the B's. Running his index finger down the column of names, he stopped at Brown, Larry. It was a longshot, Wassmuth knew, but it seemed as though he had lived off a steady diet of longshots since he had been a priest.

He punched out the number. As the phone rang, he breathed, "Be there, Larry. Be there. Please."

Someone picked up on the other end.

"Hello, is Larry Brown home?"

"Just a moment," the woman said.

Wassmuth clenched his fist and shook it in front of him.

"Hello," greeted the familiar, rugged voice.

"Larry! This is Bill Wassmuth. I need a miracle." His eyes shone with the anxiety and excitement building within him.

"Miracles are more your line of work than mine, Bill," the well-known north Idaho businessman said, laughing.

"I'm calling in the favor you once said you owed me," the priest countered, matching Brown's laugh with one of his own. Wassmuth had performed a funeral service for Brown's nephew a few years back. The grateful Brown said that if the priest ever needed anything he should let him know.

"Sure. What is it?"

"I need your private jet today. I've got to get the Governor here for the Celebration."

Brown paused, long enough to cause Wassmuth to nearly pass out from holding his breath.

"Shouldn't be a problem, Bill. It's parked out at the airport."

"Great," Wassmuth said.

"You going to need a pilot?" Brown asked, a smile in his voice. "Or are you going to fly it yourself?"

"I'll need a pilot," Wassmuth answered, tentatively. "But, I don't have any money to pay him."

"Not to worry. The pilot is part of the deal."

Wassmuth sat back in his chair. "Thanks, Larry. I'll call you back with the instructions for where your man needs to pick up the Governor."

Wassmuth hung up, and quickly called the Governor's aide to confirm everything. Then he phoned Brown back to complete the arrangements.

That done, Bill Wassmuth sat quietly for a moment. He realized this was probably the last time today he would have a moment to relax and gather his wits.

While staring off into nothingness, thoughts running around inside his head like wild horses, his eyes focused on the stuffed giraffe that sat on his bookshelf. Next to the stuffed animal was a certificate proclaiming Bill Wassmuth a member of the Giraffe

Project for the courage he had exhibited in sticking his neck out for human rights.

Wassmuth felt more proud of this honor than any he had received. Based in Washington state, the Giraffe Project was comprised of famous, wealthy and concerned citizens who believed torpor and passivity was a disease that could one day lead to the loss of the American liberties. The Project recognized people like Bill Wassmuth who had the courage to take risks for something they believed in—social entrepreneurs they called them. The Giraffe Project used the media to tell the stories of these men and women—known as giraffes—who stuck out their necks to make their world a better place. Others who'd been honored were a housewife who gave emergency shelter to 23 refugee orphans, a waitress who braved oncoming trucks and threats of violence to stop toxic waste dumping in her Tennessee community, a Hiroshima survivor who stood up to threats and ostracism to speak out against the arms race, and a successful executive who left comfort and security to gamble his life savings to create a commercial farm and a lot of jobs in the South Bronx.

Bill Wassmuth pushed slowly up from his desk chair, and walked over to the bookshelf. He touched the velveteen neck of the stuffed giraffe as he read from the certificate.

> The Giraffe Project herewith declares Father
> Bill Wassmuth to be a Giraffe whose
> courageous actions illumine all our lives
> making manifest the truth
> that people who believe in themselves and care
> for others can meet any challenge life presents.

Reading the words on the certificate caused him to reflect for a moment about how far he had come in his personal growth to win this award, how far he had traveled from his days of hoping things around him would somehow magically change. He had been transformed by the experiences of getting a Masters Degree in a personal growth-oriented program at Seattle University, and by serving as spokesperson of the Task Force. Not until the latter had he known first hand the possibilities for a community that honored *all* its citizens, or understood the gifts every citizen enjoyed when their community valued diversity and difference.

Wassmuth checked his watch. Nearly eight o'clock, time to go. He stepped out of his office, and walked quietly into the church sanctuary. He felt refreshed and renewed, and ready for the day that stretched out in front of him.

* * *

Bill Wassmuth had never seen so many members of the media in one place. There appeared to be at least two hundred newspaper, magazine and radio reporters, and television crews swarming like wasps in front of the bandstand in the City Park. The grass around the bandstand was a snarl of cables and wires, and the podium was packed with microphones and cassette recorders. Only a few participants in the Celebration had arrived for the festivities, mostly groups and families who came early to spread blankets directly in front of the bandstand.

Wassmuth spotted Dave Peters, Task Force member and a

teacher at a local grade school, circulating among the legion of reporters. The priest approached the mob of media representatives, and called out to Peters. The overweight, dark-haired Peters took leave of the media crowd, and chugged over to Bill.

"How's it look?" Wassmuth asked.

"This is *wild*," Peters answered, excitement nudging past his normal quiet tone, his face shining with perspiration. "I feel like a press agent for a presidential candidate."

"Let's hope that more than a few people show up today," Wassmuth added. "Be embarrassing if the press outnumbers the crowd."

"Probably wouldn't be the first time."

Panic captured Wassmuth's face.

"It'll be fine," Peters assured, knowing Wassmuth's proclivity for worry.

Wassmuth desperately wanted the Human Rights Celebration to succeed. He was also anxious that members of the Aryan Nations might disrupt the proceedings. More than anything he wanted to avoid a violent confrontation between the people gathered in the City Park and the Aryans. He would never forgive himself if someone got hurt, or even killed.

"I hope the police can keep order today, Dave."

"Larry Broadbent told me Sheriff Merf Stalder has brought in peace officers from as far away as Lewiston to help out."

Wassmuth was about to add something when he was approached by Jerry Jaeger. Jaeger was publicity director and co-owner of the Coeur d'Alene Resort, the recently completed high-rise complex of hotel rooms, upscale shops and restaurants, located on the lakefront adjacent to the City Park.

"This is exciting," Jaeger exclaimed, snapping his fingers as if keeping time to a jazz tune.

Wassmuth smiled. It made him feel good the management of the Coeur d'Alene resort, originally part of the group that implored the Task Force to cease confronting the human rights issue because it created bad publicity for the area, was reacting positively to today's festivities. Wassmuth decided to have some fun with it.

"You know, Jerry, your hotel is going to be the backdrop for worldwide media coverage today."

"It's terrific. What can we do for *you*?"

"I hadn't really thought about it…"

"C'mon, there must be something," Jaeger pressed.

Wassmuth glanced at the hotel. A smile came slowly to his face. "How about a night in the Hagadone Suite."

Dave Peters raised an eyebrow. "The honeymoon suite? An interesting request for a priest."

The Hagadone suite was located on the top floor of the eighteen story hotel. It had fifteen-foot picture windows, cathedral ceiling, and spacious decks, on one of which was an outdoor hot tub. There was also a glass-bottom swimming pool above the party room. At night you could sit in the hot tub under the stars and see down the entire length of Lake Coeur d'Alene.

"It's yours," Jaeger said.

"We better get moving," Dave Peters advised, taking Wassmuth by the arm. "A lot of people want to interview you."

"Remember to position yourself so that the hotel is in the background, Father Bill," Jaeger called with a laugh.

"And you remember to get the hot tub ready for me," Wassmuth said over his shoulder.

Wassmuth followed Dave Peters to the bandstand.

"Not often a guy gets to stay in a $1500-a-night suite," Wassmuth offered, with a sly grin. "I'm going to ask my sister and her husband from Portland to spend the night there with me."

Peters smiled. "Figures. You're the straightest guy I've ever met."

Wassmuth laughed.

"Let's meet the press," Peters instructed. "First up is the 'Today Show'"

Wassmuth shook his head in amazement. This sure was a long way from Greencreek, Idaho, population 30.

Peters lead Wassmuth to where the "Today Show" crew was gathered.

For the next two hours, until 11:30 when the Celebration program was to begin, Dave Peters escorted Bill Wassmuth from one group of reporters to the next. After the first few interviews, Wassmuth operated as if in a trance as he fielded the repetitive questions. "Was he afraid of a violent confrontation between his group and the Aryans?" "What was the Task Force trying to accomplish by scheduling the Human Rights Celebration on the same weekend the Aryans were holding their annual World Congress?" "What was the overall purpose of today's Celebration?" "Had the Task Force made any difference in changing the public image of Kootenai County?"

Bill Wassmuth had just finished an interview with "Good Morning America" when he was called aside by Dave Peters.

"There's a guy who says he has to talk with you," Peters petitioned.

Wassmuth noted the grave look on Peters' meaty face. "Who is it?"

"Over here."

Dave Peters lead Wassmuth to a quiet spot in back of the bandstand. They were met by a tall, deceptively-strong-looking man in a gray suit, white shirt and green tie. He wore sunglasses, and his jaw muscles jumped every few seconds.

"Bill, this is Steve Hanford of the FBI," Peters said.

Wassmuth had dealt with many law enforcement officers since becoming spokesperson for the Task Force, yet an FBI agent still gave him a strange flutter in his stomach.

"What can I do for you?" Wassmuth asked.

The blond FBI agent produced an 8x10 manila envelope, and handed it to the priest.

Wassmuth opened it and withdrew a glossy photograph of an extremely intense-looking man with dark hair and full beard, and coal black eyes that reflected the flash of the camera.

"Have you ever seen this man, Father Wassmuth?" Hanford asked.

Wassmuth studied the photo. "Not in person, but I've seen pictures of him in the paper. It's David Dorr."

"Then you know Dorr has been living in the area for about two years, and spends most of his days out at the Aryan Nations compound. He has recently been appointed the new chief of security for the Aryan Nations."

"I appreciate the information," a puzzled Wassmuth responded.

"There's more," the agent went on. "Dorr used to be a law enforcement officer in San Jose, California. He's considered extremely dangerous, so we're asking that you be careful. You happen to see this guy, Father Wassmuth, you contact us right away."

Wassmuth's stomach fluttered in anticipation of what was coming next.

"We have reason to believe that Dorr has made statements about whacking you," FBI Agent Hanford confirmed.

"I see," the priest muttered, fear coursing through his body. Human Rights work was sure different than hearing confession, presiding over church bingo games, and other parish duties.

"It's probably a lot of hot air," the FBI man added, "but we've learned it's best to take these things seriously."

Wassmuth nodded.

Hanford's face softened as he glanced from side to side. "Looks like you're going to have a big crowd."

"That's right," Dave Peters seconded.

The FBI Agent pulled off his sunglasses, and looked Wassmuth dead in the eyes. "Hope everything goes off well for you today, Father."

"Appreciate it," Wassmuth answered.

"I'll be around if you need me," the FBI man finished.

Wassmuth handed him back the manila envelope containing the photo of David Dorr. "Thanks," the priest said.

Once the FBI Agent walked away, a shaken Bill Wassmuth
followed Dave Peters around to the front of the bandstand. There
were more interviews to complete.

By the time Tony Stewart stepped up to the microphone to open
the program, the crowd in the park had swelled to over a thousand.
The atmosphere was a festive one, people of different colors and
religions and beliefs mixing together in harmony and joy.

Stewart introduced Governor John Evans, who gave an excellent
speech, lauding the efforts of the Task Force in support of Human
Rights. Representatives of the governors of Washington, Oregon and
Montana—only Wyoming had not responded to the Task Force's
invitation to participate—read messages of support.

Then it was Wassmuth's turn. He felt a twinge of nervousness as
he stepped up to the podium and gazed out over the large crowd. He
also enjoyed a sense of satisfaction at seeing the diversity of people
in attendance. It looked to him like a beautiful tapestry of different
colors and ethnic backgrounds.

Wassmuth began by discussing the history of the Aryan Nations'
involvement in Kootenai County, the formation of the Task Force,
and the importance of today's Human Rights Celebration. About
halfway through his ten minute talk something gave him a start.
Towards the rear of the crowd, amid a cluster of oak trees, stood
several men in camouflage fatigues. Even from where he was
located, some five hundred feet away, Wassmuth saw clearly that
each of them wore the familiar green berets with the red and blue
Aryan Nations swastika on the front. They were hard-looking, their
faces somber and clenched. They had apparently come to keep an

eye on the gathering, and to protest against what this celebration stood for.

Standing on the podium, delivering his speech, Wassmuth knew deep in his bones that this Celebration was a turning point, not only for the Task Force, but also for the Aryan Nations. TV cameras fixed on him, standing behind the myriad of cassette recorders and microphones, Wassmuth was convinced that the Task Force had taken the media initiative away from the Aryans. His instincts told him that from here on the influence and presence of the Aryan Nations in north Idaho was going to diminish, and that of the Task Force was going to increase.

Wassmuth wound down his speech with the thought that had become more and more apparent to him over the past several months, and was the theme of his work with the Task Force.

"Saying 'yes' to human rights is the best way to say 'no' to prejudice," Bill Wassmuth proclaimed.

He stepped away from the podium to a groundswell of applause and cheering. Before the applause and cheering died away, another sound began reverberating around the park. What began as a quiet, measured chant soon built until the entire multitude was on its feet, many people pumping their fists into the air in time to the rhythm of what they were shouting.

"YES . . . YES . . . YES . . . YES," the crowd chanted, louder and louder, until it became a deafening, joyous and sweet sound that echoed off the concrete walls of the nearby Coeur d'Alene Resort, reaching all the way to the eighteenth floor, to the honeymoon suite Wassmuth would be occupying sometime in the future with his sister

and brother-in-law.

The chant was picked up by those on the podium, including the Governor. *"YES . . . YES . . . YES . . . YES."*

The crowd speaking in one voice for human rights brought tears to Wassmuth's eyes; he was having difficulty seeing the crowd. He rubbed a knuckle into his eyes. Able to see again, he focused on the knot of sullen and angry Aryans standing among the oak trees. He could not help but contrast them to the joyous group affirming the rights of *all* people, regardless of color, religion or sexual preference.

Wassmuth stepped down from the podium as Norm Gissel began reading some of the resolutions from the various city and county governments throughout the Northwest proclaiming their support of human rights.

He checked his watch. It was nearly three o'clock. He had to get to St. Pius to perform a wedding.

"I should be back in about an hour," Wassmuth told Marshall Mend, standing off to one side of the speaker's platform.

"Ah, you Catholics," Mend kidded. "An hour for a wedding... We Jews spend half a day getting hitched."

"So how come we have a lower divorce rate than you do?" Wassmuth tossed, as he leaned into a walk.

"The threat of purgatory keeps unhappy Catholics together," Mend called, letting go his booming laugh.

Wassmuth beat it to the parking lot. Driving up the hill towards St. Pius, he noted the jet crossing the cloudless sky like a needle on a blue cloth. Governor John Evans was on his way to Burley in Larry Brown's plane.

"Thanks, Larry," Wassmuth mouthed.

Despite the excitement that lay in his stomach like a hand vibrator, Bill Wassmuth did his best to give his full attention to performing the wedding ceremony. The ceremony completed, he bid his best wishes to the bride and groom and their respective families, before dashing into the dressing room to remove his clerical collar. He slipped into an open-collared white shirt, and donned his black suit jacket. He jumped into his car and drove quickly down the hill, across town, back to City Park. On the way he was once again plagued by the fear that the Human Rights Celebration would somehow explode into a violent confrontation between those at the park and the several Aryans attending the celebration. If that should happen, Wassmuth knew, there would be no stopping the two hundred or so neo-Nazis gathered at the Hayden Lake compound from rushing into Coeur d'Alene. It could be a bloodbath. The priest even caught himself questioning his decision of suggesting to the Task Force that the Celebration be held on the same weekend as the Aryan Congress.

He was calmed somewhat upon arriving back at the park and seeing the fun-filled faces of those singing along with Rosalie Sorrels, a folk singer from Boise. The Aryans remained near the back of the crowd, except for a burly man in camouflage pants and White Power T-shirt that accentuated his rotund belly, who was stationed in front of the podium. His back to the stage, he peered through reflector sunglasses at the crowd. Wassmuth found himself chuckling. If not so hateful and violent, neo-Nazis and fascists would be laughable.

Wassmuth spotted Larry Broadbent standing nearby. Broadbent was in uniform, part of the Sheriff Department's show of strength to dissuade anyone, Aryans or otherwise, from starting trouble.

"How's it been going?" Wassmuth asked.

"Couldn't be better," Broadbent answered, proudly. He joined in the applause for Rosalie Sorrels, who had completed her final number.

Both Wassmuth and Broadbent turned their attention to the podium. Idaho State Representative Jeanne Givens, member of the Coeur d'Alene Indian Tribe, stepped to the microphone. Givens introduced the next act, the Hmong Asian dancers.

"What do you hear from the Aryan compound?" Wassmuth asked.

Broadbent removed his reflector sunglasses. "We've got over 200 officers placed strategically out there so no one can enter or leave the compound without us knowing about it. In addition we've recorded the license number of every car or truck that has gone in or out of the place for the past three days."

"Good," Wassmuth said. "What do your people report going on out there?"

"Butler, David Duke, Tom Metzger, John Ross Taylor, Robert Miles and the other leaders held a press conference earlier this afternoon," Broadbent explained, keeping his eyes on the Asian dancers, "that drew most of the media from here, like iron filings to a magnet."

Wassmuth shook his head. "Guess we had to figure as much. Nazis seem to hold a certain macabre curiosity. I couldn't believe the

New York Times did a two page feature article on Butler and the Aryans last week."

A small smile tugged at the corners of Broadbent's mouth. "The good news is that most of the reporters and news crews came back here."

"Maybe there's hope for what we're trying to do, after all."

Wassmuth stood next to Larry Broadbent and watched the next couple of acts. The most colorful and interesting to Wassmuth was the group of Coeur d'Alene Indian dancers and drummers dressed in native garb. They put on an energetic, exciting show. At one point the Indians formed into a circle and performed a dance signifying the unity of man with nature. This spiritual, energetic and symbolic dance infected the crowd with enthusiasm. Reporters closed in around the Native American dancers with cameras and tape recorders. The Coeur d'Alene Indian dancers spontaneously guided the reporters into the center of the circle. Within moments all of the reporters were inside the circle, dancing along with the Indians.

The crowd loved it; most people clapped along. Wassmuth, tapping his toe to the rhythm, felt especially pleased by the participation and success of the Coeur d'Alene Indian dancers. He thought back to the day that he, Marshall Mend, Skip Kuck and Norm Gissel visited the Tribal Council offices. Since then, the Coeur d'Alene Tribe had become extremely active on the Task Force, ready to stand shoulder-to-shoulder with the other members in the struggle for human rights.

The dancers gave way to Lawrence Arripa, Coeur d'Alene tribal story teller. Arripa stepped to the microphone and began spinning a tale about the ancient, mythical times of Lake Coeur d'Alene.

Wassmuth was struck by how similar Indian mythology was to ancient Christian mythology. He was trying to recall the metaphor from the Bible that closely resembled the story Arripa was telling, when Tony Stewart approached him.

"We've got problems, Bill," a nervous Stewart said.

"What is it?"

"Come over here for a moment." Stewart beckoned furtively with his hand for Wassmuth to follow.

The two men moved through the throng of people, to a relatively quiet spot beyond the basketball court.

"A group of college kids from Montana here for the celebration want to drive out to Hayden Lake and demonstrate at the front gate of the Aryan Nations compound," Stewart reported.

"They *what*?" a shocked Wassmuth asked.

"They want to demonstrate against white supremacy."

"Damn. They haven't gone yet, have they?"

"I asked them not to drive out there until you had a chance to talk with them."

"Thank God," Wassmuth breathed. "Where are they?"

"In the parking lot."

"Let's go," Wassmuth said. He followed Stewart to a parking lot jammed with cars.

Wassmuth saw right off that these college kids were anything but trouble-makers. There were five in all, clean-cut, and, as evidenced by them driving several hundred miles to be at the Celebration today, strongly interested in the issue of human rights. Their leader was a twenty-year-old University of Montana senior, Jack Grogan.

"I'm Bill Wassmuth," the priest said, before making the rounds with handshakes.

"Great speech," the dark-haired, huskily built Grogan offered.

"Thanks," Wassmuth added, perfunctorily. "Look, I've come to ask you not to go out to the Aryan compound."

"Why not?" Grogan asked. "We want to make a statement about our opposition to white supremacy."

"That's what we're doing *here*...Making a statement." Wassmuth extended his arm in the direction of the park. He had to work to keep his temper in check.

"What you're doing here is fine, these ethnic dances and speeches and all that," the young man continued, politely, but resolutely. "But it's not enough. We didn't want to drive all this way without letting the Aryans know how we feel about what they're doing."

Wassmuth saw in the college student a serene and steely sense of purpose that he himself possessed, a realization that seemed to irritate the priest even more.

"I don't know if you understand, but those Aryans are prone to violence, and are extremely dangerous. We have it on good authority that they are looking for some kind of excuse to cut loose against anyone involved with this Celebration."

Wassmuth leveled his eyes on Jack Grogan. "By going out there you're giving them their excuse; it'll be like throwing gasoline on a fire."

"I understand your fears," the college student responded. "But we've already made up our minds. We're going out to Hayden Lake and let the Aryans know how we feel about what they're doing."

Wassmuth looked up at the sky. He then turned to Tony Stewart, who looked as helpless as he felt.

"Do what you have to do," Wassmuth finished. "I just hope you don't screw up what we've tried to do here today."

Wassmuth turned away. He realized he had tried to guilt-trip these young men into not driving out there, but at this point he did not care. He would have done practically anything to get them to change their minds.

An angry, anxious Wassmuth, with Tony Stewart a step behind, headed back to the podium area. Despite being madder than hell at the group of students, the priest found, much to his amazement and chagrin, that he admired them for their courage. They had far more nerve than he had while in college. As a student, Wassmuth had been unconscious about human rights issues, never mind demonstrating against an avowed racist group with a record of committing acts of violence against anyone who questioned their right to maim, murder and steal.

The first thing Wassmuth did was alert Larry Broadbent to the intentions of the Montana students. Then, resolving that the matter was out of his hands, he did his best to pay attention to the rest of the afternoon's entertainment, which consisted of a Scottish Bag Pipe group, Reggae band, black pop singer, and other ethnic acts. Try as he might, however, Wassmuth was unable to keep his mind on what was occurring on the stage; he was too busy worrying about what might be happening out at the Aryan Nations compound. He remained in this state of distracted nonchalance for the next ninety minutes, in which he was unable to fully see what he was looking at, nor completely hear what he was hearing. He was that way until Larry Broadbent informed him that the students had returned from demonstrating without incident at the end of the driveway that led to the Aryan Nations compound. Wassmuth was so ecstatic that the college kids from Montana had not sparked a violent confrontation with the Aryans, he felt dancing with Broadbent.

Wassmuth was finally able to turn his full attention back to the festivities. The reggae band, comprised of five black men from Jamaica, had the crowd swaying and rocking and dancing to their music. Nearly five o'clock, this was the last act of the day.

As the day wound down, Wassmuth became filled with the sweet and good and full sensation that came with having done a tough job well. He and the others in the Task Force pulled it off; they showed the world that Coeur d'Alene and north Idaho was for everyone, not just whites.

Wassmuth was rocking back and forth in tune to the music, feeling as good as he had ever felt in his life, when Tony Stewart approached him. The Political Science professor looked like a kid padding down the stairs early on Christmas morning to discover a mountain of gifts under the tree.

"Great job, Bill," Stewart said, and embraced the priest.

"You, too," Wassmuth answered, on the break.

"This was fun. Maybe we should put one of these on every year."

Wassmuth was too tired to contemplate the idea of once again going through all the preparations that led up to today's festivities.

Besides, there was something else on his mind.

"Maybe we could do that," he said, absent-mindedly. "But I have another idea."

"What's that?"

"How about forming a five state human rights coalition?" Wassmuth posed. "Do what we're doing here throughout the northwest."

Stewart's eyebrows arched, the corners of his mouth turned down, and his face took on that quizzical, excited look Wassmuth had seen so often over the past several months. It meant Tony Stewart was giving serious thought to some idea that both fascinated and challenged him.

"We could enlist the aid of corporations, agencies and churches throughout the five state area the Aryans are claiming for their homeland," Wassmuth explained. Excitement edged past his fatigue. "We could do education, put on symposiums, investigate human rights abuses, offer victim support, work on getting legislation passed that would protect victims of malicious harassment, and stage celebrations like this one, all over the northwest.

"We could take it right to Butler and the Aryans, as well as other hate groups, wherever they try to get a foothold. We could provide community education, and help each city or town or county set up a Task Force similar to ours. Plus, we could monitor human rights abuses in the five state area, and assemble ongoing statistics about hate-related crimes that occur in the northwest."

"Bill, that's a *fantastic* idea." Stewart hopped in place, he was so excited.

Wassmuth grinned. He loved Tony Stewart's enthusiasm. Also, Bill had a deep and abiding respect for Stewart's knowledge of the political system. Tony knew his way around a state house or a county office building. The two men worked well together. Stewart moved quietly and adeptly behind the scenes, buttonholing politicians and arranging media events, while Wassmuth brought the message to the public's attention. They had proven to be an important, essential duo in the work of the Task Force.

"A Five State Coalition on Human Rights," Stewart repeated, shaking his head at the novelty of Wassmuth's idea. "It's never been attempted anywhere before. At least as far as I know."

"Sounds like a good reason to try," Wassmuth put in.

"But neither had the Task Force been tried before," Stewart finished.

Wassmuth noticed Stewart's eyes seemed focused inward, something that happened when Tony's mind was busy trying to work out the rudimentary plans for some new idea.

TWENTY-ONE

A period of calm followed the Human Rights Celebration. Bill Wassmuth believed it was brought on by setbacks the Aryan Nations suffered over the past few months. As a result of the well-publicized trial in Seattle, twenty-three members of The Order, including Randy Duey, Denver Parmenter, Richard Kemp, Bruce Pierce, David Lane and Gary Yarbrough, were convicted of murder, armed robbery, counterfeiting, conspiracy to overthrow the government and other charges, and were handed out prison terms ranging from 40 to 100 years each. Wassmuth, along with others on the Task Force, figured that The Order had been seriously weakened by the Seattle convictions, as well as by other trials around the country. Included was the Denver trial in which David Lane and Gary Yarbrough had been convicted of murdering talkshow host Alan Berg. The Aryan Nations movement was further weakened when some of its key members had been slain in shootouts with federal officials.

Beyond that, according to Larry Broadbent, the number of white supremacists moving to north Idaho had leveled off, despite Richard Butler continuing to invite people to the Nehemiah Township. Also, Broadbent reported, the number of people living at the Aryan Nations compound had decreased.

Wassmuth, Marshall Mend, Tony Stewart and the others on the Task Force felt good about the way things were turning out. They were positive they had the Aryan Nations on the run. The power of the neo-Nazis in north Idaho was on the wane.

* * *

The Subsequent Months

Larry Smith, a black man in his early fifties, pushed hurriedly through the front door of the K-Mart store in Coeur d'Alene. On his way home from work, he stopped to pick up milk for dinner. Smith hustled to the back of the store, and reached into the cooler for a half-gallon carton of milk. He turned for the cashier's desk at the front of the store, but paused. A couple of cold beers sounded good; it'd been a long hot day, and Smith had worked up a powerful thirst.

He reversed direction and made his way toward the beer cooler. He turned the corner at the end of the island full of canned goods and had to sidestep quickly to avoid walking head-on into a cart being pushed by a short, compact man with dark curly hair.

"Sorry," Smith said.

"Why don't you watch where you're goin', nigger," Larry Floyd Phillips snapped. Phillips arrived in Coeur d'Alene that day from Spanaway, Washington, to join the Aryan Nations.

The black man stopped in his tracks. "What did you say?"

"You heard me, nigger," Phillips answered, his small, closely set eyes resembling razor-slits. "Watch where the hell you're goin.'"

"You best watch your *mouth*," Smith replied, more calmly than the situation warranted.

Larry Floyd Phillips bowed his neck, and gripped the grocery cart so hard his fingers turned bloodless white.

"You watch *this*, nigger," Phillips snarled, and rammed the black man with the cart.

Taken completely by surprise, Smith was knocked backward and fell heavily against a display of panty hose. The carton of milk flew out of his hands and hit the nearby wall with a slap.

"Why don't you go back to Africa, you lousy desert dancer," Phillips called, and slammed his cart into the black man a second time. "This area is for whites only."

A stunned Larry Smith tried to scramble to his feet, but he was immediately set upon by the white man, who came at him behind flying fists and churning knees.

"You niggers are ruining this country," Phillips said from between gritted teeth.

In the front of the store, the cashier, a heavy-set woman in her late thirties, hung up the phone after calling 911 to report the incident. Her head swiveled back and forth as she traded glances between the altercation in the back of the store and the parking lot. She was greatly relieved when the Coeur d'Alene Police patrol car slid to a stop directly in front of the entrance door.

* * *

It was a quiet, warm summer night in Hayden Lake, the air smelling of pine and newly-cut grass. Wisps of smoke from neighborhood barbecues clung to the tops of dagger-shaped pines like angel hair on Christmas trees. It was an evening when men relaxed in front of television sets tuned to baseball games, while their wives sat with their tired feet propped up.

The serenity of dusk was shattered by an ear-splitting explosion at the canary yellow, cinder block Classic Auto Restoration building on Government Way. A cloud of blue smoke filled the sky immediately around the building, and the acrid odor of cordite made the rounds of the neighborhood.

Men and women, as if emerging from bomb shelters after an air raid, came tentatively and fearfully out of nearby houses. Several people walked across the street to inspect the damage done to the Classic Auto Restoration building. Though neighbors, they hardly spoke to one another. They acted as if they were expecting something like this to happen for some time. So much about their little town had changed over the past several years, things had gone on they did not understand.

* * *

Richard Butler leaned his elbows on the brown Masonite and metal table under a stand of pine trees, and squared his shoulders behind the battery of tape recorders and microphones. The covey of news reporters waited for him to resume his press conference.

Butler looked trim and fit in a tweed jacket, white shirt open at the collar, charcoal slacks, and brown leather loafers. His hair was combed, and held in place with tonic. He was seated in a metal folding chair, his back to the frame building in which his office was located. Standing in back of Butler were three burly men in camouflage fatigues and berets. Each had a baleful, scowling expression, and a holstered sidearm.

"My people were in no way responsible for the pipe bomb that exploded at the auto shop in town," Butler said, purposefully. "We'd be crazy to pull something like that around here."

Dave Oliviera, an olive-skinned reporter from the Spokane paper, raised his hand.

"It's been alleged your group is involved with the pipe bomb mailed to Judge Benson in North Dakota, the judge trying the Posse Comitatus case," Oliviera posed.

Butler's eyes narrowed, deepening the maze of spider-web-like lines that covered his face.

"What is it with you people? Where do you get your information?" Butler challenged, then caught himself. "Of course we didn't have anything to do with sending any bomb to that ZOG judge."

Oliviera wrote down Butler's answer on the small notepad he held in his left hand.

"What about Larry Floyd Phillips attacking the black man in the K-Mart store?" another reporter asked. "Phillips claimed he was on his way to join your group."

"Look," Butler answered, turning his eyes on the reporter, "all kinds of crazies show up here. We let them stay around for a few days, feed them, and send them on their way. Phillips was in no way connected to the Aryan Nations."

Butler paused, and looked hard at the reporter. "I do agree, however, that Phillips had the right to stand up for his race. I think it's a great injustice for a white Christian to be tried under this so-called Malicious Harassment Law simply for wanting to preserve his race."

Larry Broadbent observed the press conference from a spot behind the reporters. He tended to believe Butler's story that the Aryans were not stupid enough to set the pipe bomb in Hayden Lake. It would not make any sense for the Aryan Nations to antagonize the locals. He also believed Butler's statement that Larry Floyd Phillips was not attached to the Aryans, although Broadbent did feel Butler was in some indirect way responsible for inciting the attack in the Coeur d'Alene K-Mart store because of the race hate the Aryan Nations leader preached.

The Undersheriff, however, was less interested in Butler's answers to the reporters' questions than he was in the three men standing behind the Aryan Nations leader. The tallest of the three, the man with shoulder-length black hair and flowing mustache, was unknown to him; Broadbent figured him to be a recent arrival to the Aryan compound. He recognized the other two: David Dorr and Edward Hawley. Dorr, former Santa Clara County Deputy Sheriff, was the Aryan Nations' new chief of security.

Broadbent had it on good authority from the U.S. Department of Treasury and the FBI that Dorr, Hawley and other unnamed militant Aryans recently formed the Bruderschweiegen Strike Force II to fill the void caused by the death and imprisonment of members of The Order. According to the best estimates of local and federal law enforcement officials, this Silent Brotherhood Strike Force II sought to resume the war of terror begun by The Order against those who stood in the way of the Aryan Nations strategy to establish the all-white homeland in the five Northwest states, the same States in which Bill Wassmuth and sixteen other people from throughout the region were moving to set up the Northwest Coalition Against Malicious Harassment. The Undersheriff also believed this Bruderschweiegen Strike Force II, being under Richard Butler's direct authority, had access to some of the money the Aryan Nations leader received out of the $2 million never recovered from the armed robberies committed by Order members. With this money these militant white supremacists could buy the most sophisticated weapons available.

This caused Broadbent to be even more concerned for the safety of Bill Wassmuth and other Task Force members. Butler and his compatriots no doubt felt cornered by the efforts of law enforcement and human rights groups to expose them, and prevent the Aryans from carrying out their plans. This Bruderschweiegen Strike Force II, Broadbent estimated, aimed to get even for the setbacks incurred by the Aryan Nations over the past year or so, and remove Wassmuth and the others as obstacles.

No telling what they would try.

TWENTY-TWO

Athol, Idaho

Robert Pires settled nervously back into the armchair. He watched the bearded, baleful-looking David Dorr touch a ballpoint pen on the primitively-drawn sketch of several houses tacked to the wall of Dorr's living room.

"You come around this corner," David Dorr explained, his eyes constantly shifting between the sketch, and Ed Hawley and Robert Pires. "We know he's home because we've waited down the street until he finishes his nightly run."

"How can we be sure he'll be there?" the blond, stocky Hawley asked.

"You can set your watch by the guy," Dorr answered, a hint of impatience in his voice. "He jogs every night around nine o'clock; he's a fanatic about physical fitness."

Hawley leaned back in his chair, and took to playing with his wisp of a beard.

What a pussy beard, Pires thought. Put some milk on Hawley's face and let the cat lick the thing off.

"You look in the window to make sure he's in the front room," Dorr continued. "You light the fuse on the pipe bomb, and toss it through the picture window. Then run like hell. I'll be parked about a block away, at the crest of Haycraft...here." Dorr pointed to the upper right section of the sketch.

"I know exactly where that is," Hawley piped in. "My mother

lives right up the street from Wassmuth."

"We have another piece of business to discuss," Dorr picked up, as if not hearing Hawley. "Ed Shray."

A shiver ran up Robert Pires' spine, and the hair on the back of his neck came to attention. He ran a hand nervously through his brunette hair, then flipped the ends, so they lay on his shoulders. Sure he believed in the ideals of the Aryan Nations; nobody knew more than he did that the niggers and spics and Jews were ruining this country. Shit, he was from Baltimore. His hometown had been transformed into a bleeding pus sore by the Blacks and Hispanics. The city was a war zone, Mau-Mau meets Puerto Rico. Minorities destroyed or burned down public housing projects as fast as the city built them. Urban renigger Pires called public housing. What few jobs available in Baltimore were awarded to blacks, Hispanics and women under Affirmative Action. If there was anything racist and sexist, Affirmative Action was, Pires believed. He moved to north Idaho to get away from his crime- and drug-infested hometown after having read Reverend Richard Butler's newsletter about an all-white homeland centered in north Idaho. In the several months he had been out here, Pires came to see the benefits of associating only with other whites. He was committed to do everything he could to protect the white race from being overrun by the kikes and the mud people. Call people names, rough somebody up, yeah, but Dorr was talking about *killing* people. The crazy bastard was plotting to blow Father Bill Wassmuth to smithereens, and off Ed Shray. Ed Shray! Hell, Shray was one of the members of the newly formed Bruderschweigen Task Force, like himself and Hawley. Robert Pires never bargained for anything like this. The ZOG system cooked people who committed murder.

"Why Wassmuth?" Pires asked.

"It's been decided that if we take him out the Task Force will fall apart," Dorr explained.

"When do we get Wassmuth?" Ed Hawley asked.

"Within the next couple of weeks... I'll let you know," Dorr added.

Pires understood why Dorr was being vague. Order member Tom Martinez had turned police informant, and was the primary reason Robert Mathews was killed in the firefight with federal agents on Whidbey Island. Martinez was also the main government witness in the trial that sent over two dozen Order members to prison for conspiracy, armed robbery and counterfeiting. Since then the Aryan Nations members had become extremely careful about who among them could be trusted. Dorr knew the government probably had planted other informants within the Aryan movement, and the bearded ex-cop would wait until the last minute to announce the time of the operation. Most likely he would wait until he was in the car with Pires and Hawley, on the way to whack Wassmuth, so there would be no chance that either of them could phone or otherwise tip off their police contact as to what was going down.

"What about Shray?" Hawley persisted.

Dumb shit, Pires thought. Ed's too damned eager for his own good. They're going to think *he's* a freakin' informant.

Dorr's dark eyes glittered and a smile played on his lips. "Soon," he said. "We're gonna kill that race traitor, and serve up his head as an offering for Bob Mathews. Although it'd take a hundred Ed Shrays to make up for Bob Mathews."

"Kill someone?" Robert Pires thought aloud, then caught himself.

David Dorr looked at him with understanding. "It's always hard the first time, Bob. For all of us."

Behind his bored and detached look, Robert Pires was nervous as hell. He knew he could never kill anyone, and was frantically trying to figure a way out of this. Going to the police was out; Dorr and Hawley, and their wives—Debbie and Olive—watched him at all times. Plus, he had no car, and was stuck out here in the middle of nowhere with these people. The only time he left was with the rest of them, when they went shopping, or attended meetings or services at the Aryan Nations compound. So Pires figured he would have to play along until he could make his break. He desperately hoped that happened before David Dorr forced him to kill someone.

Just then Debbie Dorr leaned into the living room. "Dinner's ready," she announced, and brushed her long, wavy, straw-colored hair out of her eyes.

"Call the kids," David Dorr answered. He removed the push-pins from the wall, and rolled up the drawing of Father Bill Wassmuth's house and neighborhood. "We'll read tonight's Bible passage in here."

Debbie disappeared back into the kitchen.

The strange, inconsistent logic of these people began to get to Pires. One minute they were talking about killing a priest, and decapitating one of their own members, the next they are reading from the Bible.

TWENTY-THREE

Bill Wassmuth jogged effortlessly along the middle of deserted Haycraft Street. Not many cars traveled this quiet residential street at ten forty-five at night.

He thought to himself that he loved this place as he bent into the long grade that would take him to St. Pius X Roman Catholic Church. He breathed deeply of the clean, sharp, pine-scented mountain air. Wassmuth mused to himself that people come from all over the world to visit north Idaho, and he lived here.

The forty-five year old priest turned his bearded face towards a sky afire with stars. Wassmuth felt light, lean and strong, and had the sensation that he could stay with the plane of the asphalt and run right up into those stars. He loved being in good condition, something new for Wassmuth, who kicked a twenty year smoking habit six months earlier. In those six months he shed forty pounds and four inches off his waist.

Wassmuth picked up his pace as he moved up the hill. The lights of downtown appeared above the tops of the pine trees, resembling a box of diamonds under a jeweler's light. Beyond the town, spread out for thirty miles in a southerly direction like a sleeping black serpent, lay Lake Coeur d'Alene. Platinum specks dotted the lakeshore, lights of waterfront homes.

Wassmuth sprinted the final fifty yards to the church, whose steeple was silhouetted against the dark sky. Dedicated the previous year, St. Pius X was the church built under Bill Wassmuth's watch.

He guided the fund-raising committee, worked out every building detail with the architects, and oversaw the placement of practically every brick, steel member and yard of concrete. To Wassmuth the new church was a symbol of the changes that occurred in St. Pius X parish since he assumed his pastoral role, seven years earlier. In that time the number of families in his congregation had grown from 400 to 800, and the parish was transformed into a vibrant spiritual, educational and community center.

Wassmuth raced past the church, beyond the aqua-colored ranch-style house that served as St. Pius' rectory and his residence. He slowed to a walk halfway down the block, and made a wide U turn in the middle of the street. Hands-on-hips, chest heaving as he strained for air, and eyes cast upward, Wassmuth cooled himself out by walking along the middle of the street, past ranch-style houses that lined the street.

Wassmuth did some stretching exercises before entering his house through the unlocked back door. He chugged up the short stack of stairs, and paused in front of the kitchen sink. He quickly downed two glasses of water, then headed into the living room. He removed the jacket of his blue jogging suit, and tossed it over a nearby chair. He grabbed the newspaper, *The Coeur d'Alene Press*, and flopped down on the black and rust poof pillow, a five-foot-wide fabric filled with chunks of styrofoam. Before turning his attention to the newspaper, he absentmindedly pointed the remote at the television, and pressed the power button. The television clicked on, producing the image of a man and a woman. Wassmuth leaned back to enjoy his nightly, post-jogging ritual of watching the eleven o'clock news while simultaneously reading the newspaper.

His full attention was drawn to the television when the well-groomed newscaster began talking about Reverend Richard Butler's most recent nationwide call for whites to move to north Idaho. The news item did not particularly bother Wassmuth—Butler had been advertising for white supremacists to move to north Idaho for years—nor was he concerned by the twenty seconds of air time given to the envenomized chief of the Aryan Nations. What irked Wassmuth was the station's use of the stock footage of a cross burning they had employed to introduce every story they had done on the Aryan Nations for the past five years. No matter how bland or repetitious the story, there would always be the burning cross, surrounded by a dozen or so men in white robes, arms extended in the Nazi-like salute. In Wassmuth's view, showing the burning cross was overly dramatic, and tended to draw more attention to the inhabitants of the Aryan Nations compound than they deserved.

Wassmuth turned his eyes back to the newspaper. While studying the paper, he patted the top of his curly blond hair. The blond hair was his; the curls he got from the hair salon.

He finished reading the newspaper the same time the newscast wound down. Wassmuth pointed the remote control at the television and cut the power. He folded the newspaper before dropping it into the wooden magazine holder next to the chair.

He was about to head off to bed when he remembered the call he needed to make. He picked up the phone and punched out the familiar number. His call was answered after the second ring.

"Whattya say, Danny? How's Seattle treatin' you?"

"Wet as always," fellow priest Danny Sheehan answered. The two met fifteen years earlier at Seattle University, where they were enrolled in the Masters of Religious Education program. They became close friends over the years.

"I tried phoning you this afternoon. You out saving souls?"

"Don't know if I was saving souls or losing my mind," Sheehan answered, with a laugh.

"Thought they were synonymous."

"Believe you have something there," Sheehan responded. "Still jogging every night?"

"Just got through. You know me. I'd rather burn out than rust out."

"Not me."

Wassmuth smiled. The only exercise the overweight, heavy-smoking Sheehan managed was pushing out of his favorite easy chair to plunder the refrigerator.

"About me coming over there Thanksgiving, Danny..." Wassmuth began. He and Sheehan had talked about Wassmuth making the drive to Seattle for the long Thanksgiving weekend. "I'm going to Greencreek to visit my mother."

Wassmuth's father passed away the previous Memorial Day, and his mother was having a hard time coping with the loss. She was depressed and lonely, and Wassmuth was worried about her.

"I'd love to see you, Bill, but I understand."

"Let me see what develops. I'll let you know." Wassmuth changed position in the chair, so he was facing the picture window. He thought he saw something move near the cluster of bushes at the corner where the two streets intersected. He looked more closely. All he saw this time were deserted streets, and bushes weaving in the wind.

He had settled back into the chair when the explosion rocked his house on its foundation. The last thing Wassmuth heard before he was thrown against the wall was the sound of splintering glass, followed immediately by an awful groaning, screeching noise, like nails backing out of lumber.

"Bill," Sheehan yelled through the phone. "What the hell was that?"

Wassmuth recovered the phone and put it up to his ear.

"I don't know," a puzzled and shaken Wassmuth answered. A cloud of dust motes drifted into the living room.

"Hold on will you, Danny?"

Wassmuth placed the phone down and pushed to his feet. He walked tentatively into the kitchen. The door to the back landing lay splintered and shattered on the floor under the kitchen table. Glass and pieces of wood littered the linoleum floor. The kitchen walls were perforated in a hundred spots, holes the size of large coins.

Wassmuth's first thought was that the furnace had blown. However, the damage seemed too severe; it looked as though the damage had been done by shrapnel.

He peeked down the stairs. The back stairway was filled with dust or smoke, he wasn't sure which. The heavy back door had been reduced to shards of wood strips, and the walls around the landing were lacerated even worse than those in the kitchen. Much of the concrete pad outside the back door had been blasted away.

Wassmuth stepped over the wreckage for a look out the door. A large chunk of the back of his house was gone; shingles, two-by-fours, plywood, rafter beams, and window sections had been blown away. Wood and glass and tar paper was strewn all over his lawn, as well as on the lawn of the house across the street.

Wassmuth quickly surmised that his furnace had not blown; the explosion had occurred outside his house. Someone had detonated a bomb near his back door. Faced with that reality, Wassmuth slipped into a state of shock. His hands began trembling and he went weak in the legs. They had actually tried to kill him.

He turned, and, stepping over debris, made his way back to the living room. He picked up the phone.

"Danny..."

"Bill, you okay?"

"... Someone just tried to kill me."

"What?"

"I'll call you back just as soon as I find out what happened," Wassmuth finished, and hung up the phone.

He stood paralyzed for a moment, until it hit him how vulnerable he was. Lights were on, drapes were open, and he stood directly in front of the picture window. He was a sitting duck in the event they wanted to finish the job.

Wassmuth quickly turned off the living room lights, then hit the floor. He lay there, face pressed against the carpet for a few seconds, until he realized the house might be on fire.

Pushing quickly to his feet, he moved in a crouch across the darkened living room. He stepped over broken glass and splintered wood, and made his way through the kitchen. Easing down the stairs, he walked outside.

Lights were on in the house across the street. The elderly Mr. and Mrs. Sanborn were outside, looking up at their roof. Debris from Wassmuth's house, including his garbage can, had rained down on their house.

Where were the police? Wassmuth thought. Then he realized they had not had time to reach his house, even if someone had called them immediately upon hearing the explosion.

He checked the back of his house for a fire. Not finding one, Wassmuth returned to his living room. He located the phone and punched 911.

TWENTY-FOUR

Later That Night

Bill Wassmuth was extremely relieved to see Larry Broadbent, as the Undersheriff braked his car sharply to a stop in front of the priest's house. Wassmuth stood in the middle of his living room, amid broken glass and splintered wood, trying to quell the shaking that threatened to turn him into a new carnival ride. Never having had the experience of getting his house bombed, he did not know how to work himself out of it.

"Damn, Bill, I'm sorry," a sleepy-faced Broadbent said as he stepped quickly over the wreckage on the kitchen floor, and joined Wassmuth. "Got here as soon as I could."

Wassmuth's attention was pulled to the picture window. Outside lights from a trio of squad cars and a fire engine sliced up the darkness. Several of his neighbors were gathered in front of his house.

"Those no good..." Broadbent murmured, surveying the damage.

The priest felt suddenly cold. He stuck his hands in his pockets to prevent them from flying around in front of him.

"You okay, Bill?"

"Yeah, I'm okay. Just a little scared."

"I've put the word out not to notify the press until morning. Last thing you need right now is a mob of reporters asking you a bunch of questions."

"Appreciate it, Larry." Wassmuth knew he never could have

held it together for the press.

"I've notified the Feds," Broadbent added. "Inspectors from the Bureau of Alcohol, Firearms and Tobacco are driving over from Spokane. Might take them a little longer than usual because of the fog. FBI is already checking on some suspects."

Wassmuth nodded.

Two firefighters, followed by three police officers, entered the back door of the house and stepped into the living room.

"Little early for the Fourth of July, isn't it, Father Bill?" one of the firefighters, a St. Pius X parishioner, kidded.

Wassmuth managed a wan smile. "Either that or someone wanted to redecorate my house."

The other firefighter began poking around the kitchen. The firefighter spoke to one of the cops standing nearby, loud enough that Wassmuth overheard him. "Lucky he wasn't back here when the bomb went off. We would've been scraping him off the walls."

A shiver ran south from Wassmuth's shoulder blades.

"Appears as though you don't need our services," the firefighter standing closest to him said. "No fire."

"Thanks for coming, Butch," Wassmuth answered.

Wassmuth and Broadbent watched the two firefighters exit the house.

"My people will want to look around," Broadbent stated.

"Go ahead," Wassmuth said. "I'm going over to the chapel to gather my wits."

"You be all right?" Broadbent pressed.

"I'm fine."

Wassmuth walked back through the kitchen, and was about to turn towards the back stairs when he remembered something. He stepped into his bedroom, located at the rear of the house. The wall nearest his bed was shredded. Bits of broken glass and splintered wood covered his bed. The pillow on which he slept had been cut in half by a shard of glass the size of a large hunting knife. He went weak in the knees thinking what would have happened to him had he been in bed, and not on the phone with Dan Sheehan.

Wassmuth tore the bedspread off the bed and tossed it to the floor. Sitting on the bed, he reached for the phone. He withdrew his address book from the drawer of the night table and began calling other Task Force members. They had to know what happened, so they could take necessary precautions. He worked his way down the list to Marshall Mend.

Waiting for Mend to pick up the phone, Wassmuth checked his wristwatch. Three-thirty. He suddenly felt exhausted. He had been operating on adrenaline the past couple of hours. The softness of his bed, the sense of safety he felt with Broadbent and the other police officers in the house, along with talking with his fellow Task Force members, acted on him like a tranquilizer.

A groggy Marshall Mend picked up on the other end.

"Marshall," Wassmuth started, with a sense of urgency. "Turn on the lights around your house, call the sheriff and have them get someone up to your place. They just bombed my house."

"You okay?" Mend asked.

"Shaken and scared, but okay."

"You want me to come over?"

"Better stay with your family. I'm going over to the church for a few minutes, then maybe try to get some sleep before the press shows up," Wassmuth explained, his voice thick and deep with fatigue.

"You need anything, give me a call."

Wassmuth was warmed by Mend's compassion. "Thanks. I'm okay."

"Call me in the morning?"

"Sure..." Wassmuth glanced around his destroyed room. "Remember in the paper the other day Butler was quoted saying I was a Jew impersonating a priest?"

"Yeah, I do," Mend answered.

"Well, I've been a Jew less than forty-eight hours, and so far I don't like it."

Mend laughed. "Once a Jew always a Jew."

Wassmuth found himself laughing.

"See you later. And be careful, okay, Marshall. No telling what else these lunatics will try."

"I will. Goodnight, Bill."

Wassmuth hung up the phone, and returned his address book to the nightstand drawer. Pushing wearily to his feet, he walked silently out of his ruined room. He crossed the kitchen, stepped carefully down the stairs, passed one of the investigating officers, and moved along a sidewalk bathed in the portable spotlight the police had rigged. The bright light allowed Wassmuth to see the back of his house more clearly; a large section of rear wall was missing, and structural members of the roof protruded out of the eaves like compound fractures.

Bill Wassmuth walked out of the orbit of light, toward the church. He needed time alone. In a few hours the place would be crawling with reporters shoving microphones into his face, pointing cameras at him, and asking dozens of questions. He needed to be at his best, for himself, and for the Task Force. Not once since he had been spokesperson for the Task Force had he let anger or frustration or his personal feelings about the Aryan Nations get in the way of the message about the value of upholding the human rights of everyone. He stayed with the positive, having decided long ago that affirming rather than attacking was the most effective way to combat the hate and racism spewed out by Butler and the other Aryans. Probably more than any other single strategy, the tactic of continually affirming the positive attracted people to the Task Force and its cause, and swayed public opinion solidly against the Aryan Nations. Which was why he did not want to be frazzled or full of rage when the reporters arrived.

He stepped through the unlocked door that opened directly into the meditation chapel. A small room, the chapel contained several chairs with padded kneelers, and a miniature altar.

Wassmuth twisted the rheostat switch until the recessed canister-style lights came on low, and the room was bathed in a soft gold. He took one of the front seats. He knelt and said a few prayers, before returning to a seated position. He placed his hands on his thighs, palms upward, and closed his eyes. He focused on his breathing, and tried to clear his mind. It was difficult. Thoughts moved through his head like messages trailing slow-moving airplanes. He concentrated on his breathing until a calmness slowly seeped into him, like cool spring water running quietly into a deep well. Calmness started in his feet, and moved up his body, to the top of his head, pushing the tension up and out of him. He sat with that feeling of serene nothingness for what seemed like a few minutes but was nearly an hour. His body felt light, and he had the sensation of floating off the floor, chair and all. Coming out of it, he felt refreshed and clear, as if some other power had kicked in. He sat for a few more minutes, eyes focused on the simple brass cross on the wooden altar.

"Help me be strong, Father," he said.

Wassmuth stood and made his way quietly out of the chapel. The sky over the mountains to the west hinting of dawn, it felt cooler than it was earlier when he walked from his house to the church. He turned the corner and stepped across the dew-dampened lawn to his house. He passed the police crew, still busily searching around the back door and in the kitchen for clues. He made his way through the debris to the front room, where Larry Broadbent was speaking with one of the other officers.

"If you don't mind I'm going to try and get some sleep," Wassmuth advised.

"Go ahead," Broadbent answered.

"Call me when the reporters get here."

"You got it."

Wassmuth walked back to his bedroom. Tossing the damaged pillow to the floor, he stretched out fully clothed on his back on the bed. Arm draped over his eyes, Wassmuth was visited by a feeling of loneliness, a sensation he was experiencing more and more lately. It was a deep-felt void of not having someone with whom he was intimately connected to help him through times like these. He swallowed hard a couple of times to hold down bitter, painful tears welling up inside him. He finally drifted off into sleep.

* * *

Wassmuth thought he handled himself well through the opening barrage of questions tossed at him by the horde of television, radio, newspaper and magazine reporters that descended on his house at eight o'clock that morning. The interview migrated from his backyard—his severely damaged house the background—to the ruined kitchen, then to his bedroom, the backdrop the shattered wall behind his bed. The reporters repeatedly tried to trick him into saying the bombing was the work of the Aryan Nations, and that Richard Butler was behind this attempt on his life. Sticking to what he knew, Wassmuth avoided laying the blame on anyone.

With the departure of the reporters and news teams, the priest spent the balance of the morning talking with police, and visiting with friends and Task Force members who stopped by to offer him support. He also tried to clean up some of the wreckage. At one point, early in the afternoon, about a dozen area ministers arrived to express their solidarity through prayer. The subsequent ceremony in the meditation chapel was particularly touching for Wassmuth; the group of clergy formed a circle, held hands, and prayed with the Catholic priest for more than thirty minutes.

It was not until later in the day, when a lone newspaper reporter stopped by, that Bill Wassmuth's fatigue and fear finally got him into trouble. The reporter arrived as the priest was seated on the back steps of his house, eating the lunch his neighbors had prepared. The neighbors were gathered around Wassmuth.

"I thought you should know, Father Bill," the newspaper reporter said, as he approached Wassmuth and the others, "that I just got back from the Aryan Nations compound. Butler called the paper earlier today. He said he was going to release a statement to the press about the bombing of your house."

"And?" Wassmuth asked. Anger built within him at the mention of Butler's name. Though he had refused to say it publicly, Wassmuth had little doubt Butler's people had tried to kill him. For that moment, however—being still in shock, and fatigue gnawing away at the edges of his good judgment—Wassmuth momentarily forgot he was talking with a reporter.

"Butler stated that the bombing of your house was a lawless, tragic and cowardly act," the reporter said, watching Wassmuth carefully for some reaction.

"Big of him," Wassmuth muttered.

"He claimed it wasn't his group that did it. He said they'd be crazy to do something that would so obviously be blamed on them."

"That right?" Wassmuth answered, his voice dripping with contempt.

"Butler suggested that maybe the Anti-Defamation League bombed your house in order to turn the feelings of the community against the Aryan Nations."

"*The ADL bomb my house*?" Wassmuth posed, a sarcastic smile turning his lips white.

The reporter paused, then added, "Butler proposed that a reward fund be established, to be given to anyone who comes forward with information leading to the arrest of whomever bombed your house."

Wassmuth shook his head in astonishment.

"Butler even donated a thousand dollars to start the reward fund," the reporter finished, with a wry smile.

Wassmuth's face and ears burned.

"He going to use counterfeit money to pay the reward?" Wassmuth snapped.

The reporter smiled, and waited for Wassmuth to continue.

"You know what he's trying to pull, don't you?" the priest added. "He's trying to do what he's done all along; he's trying to upstage the publicity over the bombing, which is ridiculous when you consider that his people probably did this. They're the only ones who'd want to get rid of me. The Anti-Defamation League certainly wouldn't want to kill me."

All the color drained from Wassmuth's face. He opened and closed his hands, his knuckles blanching white with each fist he made. He was angry enough that if Butler were standing there he might have foregone his commitment to nonviolence and put the Aryan leader through what remained of the back wall of his house.

"Butler also suggested that you and he call a joint press conference to condemn the bombing," the reporter added.

"I won't appear in public with him... anywhere... anytime," a seething Wassmuth answered. "I don't acknowledge him. I wouldn't give him the satisfaction or credibility of appearing with him."

The reporter moved away. Wassmuth turned back to his neighbors.

After lunch, the priest worked with members of his parish who came by to help him pick up the mess both inside and outside his house. They coordinated their clean-up efforts with Larry Broadbent and the half-dozen federal firearms agents from Spokane investigating the bombing, so as not to destroy any evidence.

The federal agents quickly ascertained from the evidence that someone planted a pipe bomb near the back door of Wassmuth's house. The bomb, they surmised, was powerful enough to kill Wassmuth if he had been in his kitchen or bedroom, or anywhere in the rear of the house. Or, the agents stated, if whoever planted the bomb had thrown it through the front window rather than leaving it near the back door, Wassmuth would not be with them today.

Later that afternoon, Wassmuth helped the carpenter, a St. Pius parishioner, temporarily close up the holes in the walls, and nail a piece of plywood over the back door opening. They had just finished the job when Wassmuth was beckoned to the phone. It was his secretary, Wanda, calling him from the church office.

"Bill, there's a call for you on line one. It's from the Jewish Defense League," the woman explained.

He was familiar with the JDL from the media's coverage of their violent reprisals against people who committed anti-Semitic crimes against Jews. Wassmuth considered them a vigilante organization, hardly better than the hatemongers they battled.

Wassmuth pressed the button flashing on the phone.

"Hello?" he said.

"Father Bill Wassmuth?"

"Speaking."

"This is Zev Loren of the Jewish Defense League in New York."

"What can I do for you?" Wassmuth asked, tentatively.

"We want to express our sympathy for the bombing of your house," Loren explained. "We also wish to offer our support to you, for your work with the Task Force, and for standing up for the Jewish members of your community."

"I appreciate it."

"We also want to let you know that we believe the Aryans are a malignant tumor that needs to be eradicated."

Wassmuth listened.

"We're coming out there, Father Wassmuth, to take out the Aryan Nations in a military action."

A scene of wild, running gunfights all over north Idaho, buildings burning, and bloody corpses in the streets flashed before Wassmuth's eyes. If Marshall Mend thought the area's image had been tarnished by what had happened so far, Wassmuth figured, wait until he gets a load of this.

"Hold on," Wassmuth warned. "You do understand that what you're talking about doing goes against everything the Task Force stands for."

"Maybe you don't fully comprehend... People like the Aryans don't respect the law, nor are they ever eliminated by peaceful methods. You have to respond in kind to them."

"I don't agree. We'll beat them by focusing on the positive."

"Focusing on the positive didn't stop them from bombing your house," the caller added, convincingly. "Next time they may succeed in killing you, Father Wassmuth."

"There is no proof the Aryans did this," Wassmuth reasoned, lamely.

"We both know better than that, Father."

"I'm begging you, don't come out here. If this thing escalates into a violent confrontation, it'll only make matter worse."

Silence from the other end of the line.

"We can handle things," Wassmuth repeated. "The law enforcement agencies are doing a good job. They'll catch whoever bombed my house. And the Task Force has rallied the community against the Aryans and those like them."

"I think you're making a big mistake not accepting our help, Father," Loren said, with a note of resignation.

"I'll take my chances."

"Okay. But I want you to know that you can call us if you need us. Anytime. We can be out there with less than a day's notice."

"Thanks. I don't think I'll need you," Wassmuth said, and hung up.

He stood there, stunned.

* * *

The following morning, at his desk with the morning newspaper in front of him, Wassmuth realized the full extent of the mistake he had made in losing his temper in front of the reporter. In the article, the reporter made a big deal of Wassmuth forgoing the presumed innocent basis of the United States judicial system by accusing Richard Butler and his people of attempting to kill him. And once again Wassmuth felt as though he played into Butler's strategy of eliciting public sympathy and upstaging the Task Force in the press.

TWENTY-FIVE

For ten days after the bombing Bill Wassmuth walked around in a daze. He was plagued by fear, which he kept to himself, that they would come back and finish the job. He became more cautious in his daily affairs. He checked over his shoulder while walking down the street. He looked both ways as he stepped out of a building. He also changed some of his habits. He no longer jogged late at night. Instead he did his roadwork early in the evening, and never alone. He now locked his doors and windows.

The bombing and resultant stress produced another change in him, one far more damaging than turning cautious and locking his doors. Wassmuth began drinking to settle his nerves. Always someone to enjoy an occasional couple of beers or a mixed drink, Bill found himself with a drink in his hand almost every night. It reached the point that some of his parishioners—people close to him—took to mentioning their concerns about his drinking. As was his style, Wassmuth listened, but remained convinced his drinking was a natural reaction to the extreme stress he was under, and that it was not a problem for him or others. He was performing his priestly duties, and maintaining his demanding schedule with the Task Force.

Some of his fears were allayed when Larry Broadbent provided him police protection. Police officers were present whenever the priest gave a speech at some public function, and several times each night the interior of his house was flooded with light from a police car spotlight, as law enforcement officers conducted regular drive-by checks of his residence.

He was also comforted considerably by the outpouring of support and affection he received from the parishioners of St. Pius X and the citizens of Coeur d'Alene, and from all over the nation. Letters and phone calls came in by the hundreds. Wassmuth was most touched by the letters from students of Coeur d'Alene's Ramsay Elementary School who took it on as a school project to write him letters of support. One boy assured Wassmuth that *he* had not bombed the priest's house; another said he would like to come over and help rebuild Wassmuth's house, but, as a second grader, he was too small.

The letters and calls and visits helped Bill avoid feeling isolated, and in some measure reduced his paranoia. It was not, however, until the solidarity reception at North Idaho College that he truly stepped out of the fog and shadow of fear and shock.

Over 700 people were seated in a series of concentric circles in North Idaho College's Bonner Auditorium. Wassmuth, wearing a yellow V-neck sweater and brown slacks, was ushered into the Bonner Auditorium by Tony Stewart, Marshall Mend and Norm Gissel. The sight of all the people crammed into the room, most of whom were standing and applauding him, acted on Bill Wassmuth like a balm that drew out the poison trapped deep within him. All the anger and fear he had felt over the past ten days flowed out of him as scalding tears that filled his throat and eyes. Wassmuth had to fight to hold it together. So tired and emotional from the past week and a half, he was not sure he would be able to stop if he started crying.

Wassmuth passed many people he knew and loved as he made his way to the front of the auditorium. Mayor Ray Stone reached out and patted him on the shoulder. Skip Kuck stepped out and hugged him.

"It'll be okay," she assured.

"Thank you," he said, and stepped out of her embrace.

He took a chair in the front row, and listened while Dick Hermstad, Pastor of Trinity Lutheran Church, gave a short talk about the need for Task Force members and the community to transcend their desire to retaliate with anger and violence. Hermstad discussed the need to keep things positive and to continue stressing non-violent, peaceful measures to deal with the activities of various hate groups, including the Aryan Nations.

Governor John Evans took the microphone. He praised Wassmuth and the Task Force, and said that the State of Idaho would not tolerate the kind of violence that happened to Bill. The Aryan Nations, the Governor said, had no place in Idaho.

It was Bill Wassmuth's turn to speak. He stepped up to the microphone, and gazed out over the sea of faces. He swallowed hard several times to compose himself as he looked out over row after row of people he knew and loved, all of whom were on their feet clapping loudly, many with tears streaming down their faces. Wassmuth turned away from the microphone to clear his throat of emotion.

He turned back to the crowd. Waiting for the applause to wind down, Wassmuth was hit by a shock wave of fear and anger upon noticing Richard Butler near the back of the room. A good thirty feet from the podium, the Aryan Nations chief stood motionless, hands jammed into the pockets of his black cotton slacks, staring hard at Wassmuth.

Wassmuth drew a couple of deep breaths, and, like an animal on the alert in the face of danger, felt a sense of clarity and courage. He was completely in control of his emotions. His blood pressure kicked into high gear, and his heart beat a rhythm against the inside of his chest. Richard Butler's presence helped the priest compose himself enough to deliver the short talk he had prepared for the gathering.

"We shall go after our goals from a different perspective, now," Wassmuth explained, "knowing what it means to be vulnerable— what Jews and people of color have known all along. We feel it now, and we continue to stand alongside others who know it all the time.

"We say YES to the dignity of each person, and NO to racism and prejudice; YES to nonviolence and peace, NO to violence; YES to unity, and NO to division.

"If we care about the persecuted and the innocent, we need also to care for the persecutor and the guilty.

"We need to help everyone in this community to feel welcome in Coeur d'Alene, and want to stay here a long time."

Wassmuth finished by leveling his gaze at Butler. "Whoever bombed my house made a very big mistake, as evidenced by this gathering tonight. They have reawakened our community to the task of confronting hate related crimes, in whatever form they take."

Wassmuth turned from the podium, and took his seat. He felt good about his speech.

Later that night, upon returning to a house that had been mostly repaired in the ten days since the bombing, the priest found a single red rose taped to his back door. He carefully removed the rose, unlocked the door, and entered his house. Instead of his usual ritual of mixing himself a whiskey and water, he sat down in the living room, and held the rose close to his face. Something about the gift of the flower, and breathing deeply of its fragrance, helped him clarify what he felt since leaving the North Idaho College auditorium. As a result of the bombing, and tonight's solidarity meeting, he had undergone some deep form of surrender, an inner transformation of a magnitude he had never before experienced. He was unsure of the reason for this transformation. Had the bombing put him in touch with his mortality? Or did the blast push him into some new realm of spirituality he had only read about in theology books? Of certain things, however, he was certain: absent was the inner sense of urgency he had known most of his life; gone was the desire to control or at least influence people, places and things around him. What remained was a void that was at the same time a fullness and an emptiness, a peaceful, empowering surrender to life on life's terms. Further, all fear had left him, as had the frustrated helplessness he experienced in the days since the bombing. Both were dissipated by tonight's solidarity meeting, and by the simple, symbolic kindness of whoever left him the solitary rose. This sense of peace was different from the passivity and apathy he had known before; this was a stronger resolve than ever to fight for human rights. His commitment to the work of the Task Force had been bolstered and strengthened as a result of his brush with death. The sense of surrender he knew was something akin to an acceptance that life was a heartbeat at a time proposition, able to be snuffed out at any time by any number of events beyond his control. He understood he was unable to prevent that which was going to happen anyway, that life had its own timetable. It was a realization that caused Wassmuth to know that his only duty to himself and others was to experience life to the fullest. He needed to let himself go to his work with his parish, and to his duties with the Task Force.

Wassmuth settled into his chair and tried to figure what the Aryans' next move might be, and how the Task Force might counter it. Never in his wildest imagination would he have guessed that the Aryans were going to do to the city of Coeur d'Alene what they had done to him.

TWENTY-SIX

Robert Pires thought David Dorr looked even more intense and
dangerous than usual. Dorr's coal-black eyes were feverish-looking
in the candlelight, his straight black hair plastered down, and his face
puffy. Over the past few weeks, the Aryan Nations' Chief of
Security had worked overtime under extremely stressful conditions,
and sleep had been mostly an unavailable luxury. Dorr had been
planning and executing operations of the Bruderschweigen Strike
Force, along with overseeing the printing and distribution of
counterfeit money, the proceeds of which was to be used to purchase
weapons. Lately, however, the counterfeit scheme—a main funding
source for the Bruderschweigen Strike Force—was unraveling. Ed
Hawley, seated in the corner of Dorr's living room, staring stupidly at
the candles on the table like he was on acid, had been busted recently
trying to pass bogus $20 bills at the Eastern Washington State Fair.
Hawley broke one of the basic rules of passing counterfeit money by
trying to hit the same place twice. In addition to Hawley's arrest,
some Aryan people back east were nailed trying to pass counterfeit
bills whose origin had been traced back to north Idaho. As a result
Treasury Agents alerted the entire nation about the Aryan Nations'
counterfeit bills, putting merchants, bankers and others on notice to
watch for the bogus money.

The cash flow all but dried up, Dorr and the others were unable
to buy weapons needed to arm those attracted to the militant wing of
the Aryan Nations. Which was the reason David Dorr called this

impromptu, middle-of-the-night secret meeting.

"If we time it right," Dorr explained, his voice hoarse with exhaustion, "we can sufficiently confuse the cops so we can hit the armory and the bank without them catching on."

"The three of us are going to set bombs off all over town, *then* stick up both a bank and the National Guard Armory?" Pires asked, incredulously.

"Shouldn't be a problem," Dorr answered. "All we have to do is time the explosions right. Besides, The Order stole nearly $6 million using these same tactics. Worked for them, and it'll work for us."

Dorr stared at Pires in a menacing way that caused the latter's stomach to flutter.

"When?" Pires asked.

"Tomorrow."

Pires let out a long breath. "I guess I'd better get some sleep, then."

Pires leaned forward, readying to push out of the armchair, when Dorr reached over and touched his knee.

"Hold on a minute, Bob," Dorr instructed. "I need to talk with you, alone."

Ed Hawley got the message, and stood. He extended his arms, arched his back, and yawned. "See you guys in the morning."

"You bet, Ed," Dorr answered. "Sleep good."

Dorr watched Hawley climb the stairs and close the bedroom door behind him. His dark eyes afire, Dorr turned to Pires.

"I've been given the order to neutralize Ed Hawley," Dorr revealed.

"*What?*"

David Dorr held a finger to his lips. "Not so loud."

"*Ed?!*" Pires exclaimed. "You gotta be kidding, man."

"Certain people figure Hawley is a security risk, that he'll either do something dumb that will sink us all, or, like Parmenter and Martinez, sing like a canary to the ZOG."

Pires shook his head. Parmenter and Martinez were Order members turned police informers. Their testimony destroyed The Order. But Ed Hawley? Pires did not particularly care for the guy, whom he viewed as a country bumpkin. But kill him? Hell, Hawley had a wife and a couple of kids. Besides, Ed and Olive Hawley were dedicated Aryans. Pires then recalled Walter West, the Aryan Nations member killed by Order members. The guy's body was not even cold when another Aryan member moved in with West's wife. Maybe that was it, Pires thought, someone had his eye on Olive Hawley.

"I need to know you're with us," Dorr pressed, his wild stare locked on Pires' eyes, as if searching for any hint of hesitation.

"I'm with you," Pires responded. He knew there was no getting out of this one. Dorr was testing his loyalty to the Bruderschweigen Strike Force. Pires figured Dorr was going to order him to pull the trigger on Hawley. By killing Ed Hawley, Pires bonded himself forever and completely to the Aryan cause.

"We'd better turn in," Dorr suggested. "Tomorrow is a big day. We'll deal with Ed after the other business."

Robert Pires pushed wearily to his feet. His mind was going a mile a minute, as he tried to figure how he was going to avoid committing murder.

* * *

Coeur d'Alene

The first bomb detonated a few minutes after nine in the morning outside the Federal Building in downtown Coeur d'Alene. The blast shattered windows and did structural damage along the 4th Street side of the three story depression-era stone building. Luckily, federal employees occupying the offices closest to the street were attending a weekly staff meeting on the opposite side of the building. Otherwise some of them would have been seriously injured or killed.

In the few moments between when the stunned employees of the Federal Building attempted to figure out what happened and evacuated the building, another bomb exploded about a mile away, on the roof of a building housing a cluster of shops. Among the shops in the Gibbs Mercantile building on Northwest Boulevard was the New Era Telephone Communications Company. The owner of New Era arrived at nine o'clock, and had just poured himself a cup of coffee when the blast rocked the building at seventeen minutes after nine. Jim Boyer, owner of New Era, realized immediately that something bad occurred, but was not sure what. At first he thought the furnace in the basement of the building exploded. That was until he smelled the gunpowder. He left his store, and followed the acrid, heavy smoke to the Luggage Rack, the travel shop located down the hall. The plate-glass display windows of the shop were blown out, and merchandise lay strewn along the corridor. Boyer peered inside.

There was a hole in the far wall, next to the desk. The blast had sent several chunks of the outside wall all the way across the shop; a section was lying outside in the corridor. Boyer sighed with relief. Lohman Catron, owner of The Luggage Rack, informed Boyer the night before that he had some things to attend to on the way to work this morning and would not be in until eleven. All Boyer could think about as he turned back for his shop to call the police was that if Catron had been sitting at his desk, as he did most mornings at this time, he would be history right now.

Eleven minutes later, at 9:26, a powerful bomb exploded in back of Jax Restaurant. Jax, a popular coffee shop, was located on Sherman Avenue, about four blocks from the Federal Building. As with the other bombings, luck played favorably in preventing injuries or deaths. The blast occurred in the parking lot of the busy restaurant at the moment when no one was either entering or leaving the restaurant by the back door.

In those twenty-three minutes the quiet resort town of Coeur d'Alene was thrown into a siege mentality. Extra deputies rushed in from surrounding towns to guard public officials. Armed sentries stood strategically around various facilities, including several banks. Police patrolled the streets looking for suspects or signs of civil insurrection. The area's schools locked their doors and refused to let anyone in or out. Sealing of the schools was a reaction to the incident that had occurred some months earlier when a bomb-carrying couple, later identified as white supremacists, held a Wyoming school full of kids hostage. The incident ended when one of the bombs accidentally exploded and killed the female terrorist.

Her husband turned his gun on himself, taking his own life. In addition, several Coeur d'Alene buildings were evacuated after bomb threats were received, including the County Office Building and the Bureau of Land Management Building. People walked nervously around town, realizing that at any moment another bomb might explode. The anxiety was heightened when police discovered an undetonated bomb on the roof of the Armed Services Recruitment Offices Building, kitty-corner from the Federal Building.

Privately, Larry Broadbent blamed the bombings on the Bruderschweigen Strike Force II. His cop instincts suggested that the location of the bombs and the sequence of the blasts were meant to create a diversion. A diversion for what, Broadbent did not know. He would do better figuring it out once he learned for certain who set the bombs. Trouble was, neither his people nor the feds had been able to infiltrate the new violent arm of the Aryan Nations. The Bruderschweigen Strike Force II was most likely comprised of only a handful of people, which made it extremely difficult for law enforcement to plant an informant. Broadbent figured it would be only a matter of time before the group made a mistake. He just wanted it to be soon, before this group of hatemongers killed someone. It'd only been a matter of luck that they had not so far.

* * *

One more time Bill Wassmuth's temper spiked while he read the morning paper. The day after the bombings rocked Coeur d'Alene, throwing its citizens into a near-panic, the newspaper carried a full page interview with Richard Butler about the mysterious explosions. What frosted Wassmuth's apples was that once again the newspaper gave Butler a forum from which to spout his whining, hateful and neurotic rhetoric about how whoever had set the bombs at Wassmuth's house and the three Coeur d'Alene locations were out to discredit the Aryan Nations. What rankled Wassmuth was that the Aryan leader—he refused to refer to Butler as a minister—had the uncanny knack of making it look as though the Aryans were the victims of prejudice, instead of what they were, the purveyors of prejudice and violence. Butler, Wassmuth thought, had the ability to fall into a pile of swine swill and come out smelling like a rose.

TWENTY-SEVEN

Larry Broadbent sat quietly behind the wheel of his car. He had parked so he could see the entire parking lot of Denny's Restaurant. Three o'clock in the morning, there was not much action around the all-night restaurant.

Broadbent lit another cigarette. Despite the late hour, and having been yanked out of a sound sleep, Broadbent was excited. The late night call had come from the FBI, advising him that Robert Pires had contacted them and stated he wanted to talk about some things. The FBI suggested Pires talk with Broadbent; and Larry Broadbent had been around police work long enough to know that when someone like Robert Pires wanted to talk, you listened.

Broadbent glanced across the parking lot to the darkened side street. He could barely make out the dark blue van positioned in front of the corner house. Two FBI guys, along with a Sheriff's Deputy, waited inside the van. Backup.

Broadbent returned to scanning the parking lot and the street in front of Denny's. He did not know what kind of car to look for, nor even if Pires might be on foot. All Pires said on the phone was for Broadbent to meet him in the Denny's parking lot at three o'clock.

Broadbent sat straight up when the white Toyota pickup eased into the parking lot. He recognized the man behind the wheel as Robert Pires. The pickup nosed into a parking spot less than ten yards from his car.

"The package has arrived," Broadbent mouthed into the wire he wore. Grinding his cigarette out in the ashtray, Broadbent took a deep breath. He pushed out of his car and walked towards the pickup.

Pires stepped from the truck.

"Hello, Bob," Broadbent greeted.

"Hi," Pires answered.

Broadbent saw that Pires was nervous. He also looked exhausted, the hollow, tortured look of a man who had struggled with fear and doubt.

"Isn't that Dorr's pick-up?" Broadbent asked, motioning to the truck.

"Yeah," Pires replied, his thick mustache moving with the smile playing on his lips. "I borrowed it for the evening."

"What do you have for us, Bob?" Broadbent withdrew his pack of cigarettes from his shirt pocket and offered Pires one.

"I'd like to make a deal," Pires answered, plucking a cigarette from the pack.

"Depends on what you have for us," Broadbent continued. He lit Pires' cigarette with his lighter. "Can you help us with the bombings?"

"All of them."

"Be specific."

"Wassmuth's house, and the ones downtown." Pires drew deeply on the cigarette, while looking nervously around.

"What else?" Broadbent asked.

"Everything."

"We might be able to do something for you."

"I want protection," Pires said, quickly. "Dorr's gone nuts. First it was Shray, now he wants to knock off Ed Hawley. Shit, I could be next."

"We'll take care of you," Broadbent assured. He felt good inside. This was the break they were looking for.

TWENTY-EIGHT

Larry Broadbent rode shotgun in the speeding car, third in the line of fifteen other unmarked police cars racing along the gravel road on a cool, overcast day. This kind of blitzkrieg operation got Broadbent's blood up. It was the type of police action in which the average cop only participated a few times in his career.

Broadbent and several other officers from the Kootenai County Sheriff's office, along with nearly forty agents from the FBI, Division of Alcohol, Tobacco and Firearms, Treasury Department, Secret Service and various state law enforcement agencies, were about to raid David Dorr's house in Athol, a tiny town twenty miles outside Coeur d'Alene.

This operation was hurriedly pulled together over the past eight hours, beginning immediately after Broadbent's meeting with Robert Pires. So far it was going by the book; roadblocks had been set up on all roads leading out of the Athol area.

The white clapboard farmhouse came into view. A lone car sat out front. The place seemed quiet. This kind of operation worked best when law enforcement officers had the element of surprise on their side; by the look of things they had it going for them.

One by one the cars slid to a halt in front of Dorr's house. Agents jumped out of cars with weapons at the ready. Still no sign of life from the house.

Broadbent and the chief of the FBI detail, a blond, burly guy who could have played guard for Brigham Young University, walked in tandem toward the front door. Except for a slight dryness in his mouth, Broadbent felt neither afraid nor anxious; his confidence was bolstered by enough firepower behind him to overthrow certain third world countries.

The FBI man, gun in hand, hung back while Broadbent stepped up to the door. The Undersheriff rapped his knuckles against the wood.

The door was opened by short, stocky Debbie Dorr, dressed in jeans and a blue flannel shirt. A slight widening of her eyes was her only indication of surprise at facing the army of law enforcement officers. Debbie was whom the authorities figured would have been a leader in the Aryan Nations movement if she had not had the misfortune of being female. White supremacists relegated their women to cooking and cleaning, and serving as brood mares for the creation of new Aryan warriors.

"Mrs. Debbie Dorr?" Broadbent inquired as a matter of ceremony. "We have a warrant to search your house."

Her face tightened with rage as Broadbent held up the document.

"We also have an arrest warrant for your husband, and for Edward Hawley."

"We're coming in, now," the FBI agent standing behind Broadbent informed.

"We have nothing to hide," the woman answered.

She stepped aside. Broadbent and the FBI man, followed by several other law enforcement officers, pushed into the farmhouse. The furniture was vintage thrift shop.

The blond FBI agent returned from one of the rooms off the

living room with two people in tow. One was a pudgy, baby-faced man with a wispy beard; the other a plucky-looking woman with a round face and hard, cold eyes.

Look what we have here, Broadbent thought, recognizing Ed and Olive Hawley. This operation was netting more than he figured it would.

He quickly reviewed what he knew about the Hawleys. Ed drifted into the Aryan Nations movement in the early 1980's, still in his teens. He moved into the Aryan compound after he married Olive, several years older and mother of a five year old son who was enrolled in the Aryan Nations youth movement. Ed Hawley served as a guard during the past few Aryan Congresses, and was considered as an up and coming white supremacist warrior. He also showed up the previous August at the St. Pius parish days picnic to intimidate Marshall Mend. In addition, it was Hawley and his wife who were picked up a few months back for passing counterfeit money at the Spokane Fair.

Another agent entered the living room. He had his gun trained on David Dorr. Thirty-four year old Dorr wore a pale blue shirt with the Aryan swastika on each shoulder.

"He was out back," the agent reported.

"Anyone else around?" Broadbent asked.

"There's no one else here," Debbie Dorr said. "Robert Pires used to live here, but he took off in the middle of the night a couple of nights ago with our truck."

"Was he living here?" Broadbent asked.

"We took him in after he left the compound," Debbie Dorr

answered. "He was trying to earn enough money to move someplace back east."

Maryland, Broadbent mused, fighting off a smile. "Let's take a look around this place," the Undersheriff said, a twinkle in his eye.

"I agree," the blond FBI agent seconded.

David Dorr cut Broadbent a hard, sidelong glance. The Undersheriff had a good idea why Dorr was angry about his house being searched. If Robert Pires' information was correct, Broadbent figured they were close to something big.

TWENTY-NINE

Larry Broadbent looked as if he had just won the lottery as he stepped into Bill Wassmuth's office at St. Pius. Wassmuth heard about the raid on Dorr's house; he had no idea what the operation turned up.

"Looks like we've solved the bombing of your house," Broadbent reported.

Wassmuth sat up straight in his chair.

"Searching Dorr's house and property we discovered explosives and other material to make bombs that match the one used on your house."

"*All right*," Wassmuth said, excitedly, and waved his fist in the air.

"We also found a stash of counterfeit money and a printing press. The bogus bills match the counterfeit money that has been passed around the northwest over the last few months."

"Good."

"In addition we ran across an arsenal of automatic weapons," Broadbent reported, slowly shaking his head. "Enough guns and ammunition to equip a small army."

Bill Wassmuth felt a strange combination of excitement, relief and anxiety.

"It gets even better," Broadbent volunteered.

"That right?"

"Robert Pires told us a very interesting story about the bombing of your house. Seems Mr. Pires was one of the three people who attempted to kill you," Broadbent explained.

Wassmuth felt his stomach shrink. The Undersheriff talking about the bombing reminded Wassmuth that they had actually wanted to kill him, something he had tried to put out of his mind.

"Pires, Dorr and Hawley bombed your house," Broadbent continued. "According to Pires, the other two wanted to kill you. Pires apparently lost his nerve. He claims that when he first arrived at the compound the Aryans sold him on the idea they would never do anything as serious as kill anyone. At any rate, from what Pires tells us, the bombing of your house went down something like this: David Dorr drove Pires and Ed Hawley to a spot a couple of blocks from your house; Pires and Hawley were under Dorr's orders to wait until you were in your living room, then throw the bomb through your front window. After it went off they were to go in with an automatic weapon and make Swiss cheese out of you."

Wassmuth suddenly felt clammy. His mind recreated the image of the night of the bombing. He saw himself sitting in the living room, talking on the telephone. He imagined two figures, one of them carrying the pipe bomb, prowling around his house in the dark. He tried to consider what would have happened to him if they had carried through with their plan to toss the bomb through his front window. He thought of how the interior walls at the back of his house had been shredded, and figured he would have easily have been cut to pieces by shrapnel. He would have had no chance.

"However, upon approaching your house," Broadbent picked up, "Pires talked Hawley out of throwing the bomb through the front window. He convinced Hawley to leave the bomb near the back door of your house; that would be enough to scare you into backing out of the Task Force. Pires' reasoning was that the Task Force would fold once you were off the scene, and thus would no longer harass the Aryans."

Wassmuth's eyes widened. "The Task Force harassing the Aryans? That's a laugh."

"Shows how little they know about you, and about the Task Force. They never imagined that bombing your house would accomplish just the opposite effect, cause the Task Force and most of the community to be even more resolved to work for human rights."

"I can understand why they'd bomb *my* house, and try to scare me off," Wassmuth probed. "But why did they set those three bombs off around town?"

"Those bombings were a diversion. They planned to rob two banks, as well as the National Guard Armory. Apparently something went haywire, and they didn't do the robberies."

"They actually thought they could pull it off?" Wassmuth asked.

"They were inspired by what the Order accomplished," Broadbent explained, gravely. "Nearly $6 million in armed robberies in two years…"

"Makes sense."

"A familiar scenario. All outlined in *The Turner Diaries*."

Wassmuth nodded. *The Turner Diaries*, written by white supremacist William L. Pierce, was a novel detailing a bloody race war in the United States. The white supremacist group that precipitated the war financed itself through actions similar to those pulled off by The Order, the role model for this new group, The Bruderschweigen Strike Force II. Like Bob Mathews, the hero of the book dies a fiery death.

Wassmuth then asked the question that had been forming in his mind.

"Can you tie Butler to the bombings? Or to the counterfeiting?"

"Not so far," Broadbent said, sadly. "He's been careful to keep at arm's length from the violence and counterfeiting."

"He just preaches violence and hate. And puts others up to it."

"Ask me, the entire Aryan Nation ideology is strictly a case of, `if you don't believe in something, you'll fall for anything,'" Broadbent added, with a wan smile.

"You can say that again."

"Something positive might come out of all of this," Broadbent added. "The Aryan Nations being behind the bombings is going to seriously if not fatally hurt their movement. The entire community will turn against them. Even those who had no real feeling one way or the other will think Butler and his people ought to be run out of the state, that the Aryans are a menace to the public safety."

"You figure he's finished?" Wassmuth conjectured.

"I hope so," Broadbent answered.

"Makes two of us," a relieved Bill Wassmuth added.

THIRTY

"Any special reason you wanted to come out here?" Broadbent asked, as he steered his car along Rimrock Road in Hayden Lake.

Wassmuth trained his brown, mournful eyes on the long driveway leading from the highway to the Aryan Nations compound, hidden behind a stand of trees. Wassmuth was amused that it took Broadbent so long to inquire about his request to detour by the Aryan Nations headquarters on their way to the Spokane Airport. Broadbent was a man who respected the privacy of others, who figured people had reasons for what they did, and if it was not police business, he let them alone. Which in Wassmuth's view made Broadbent the outstanding law enforcement officer and trusted friend he was.

"Wanted to see the place one last time before we flew to New York," Wassmuth explained.

Wassmuth, Broadbent, and Mayor Ray Stone were flying to New York to accept the Raoul Wallenberg award on behalf of the city of Coeur d'Alene. Coeur d'Alene had been named the recipient of the prestigious award—named for the Swedish diplomat who saved thousands of Jews from certain extinction by the Nazis by smuggling them out of Hungary during the Second World War—for its work to guarantee the basic human rights of all of its citizens. It was especially appropriate for Mayor Stone to accept the award. He was with the first unit of American soldiers to liberate Dachau concentration camp at the close of the war. It was a scene that stayed with Stone all his life.

"I thought if I saw this place before we took off it might help me put things in perspective," Wassmuth finished. He was taken by the same sensation of being in the presence of evil he got whenever he was anywhere near the Aryan Nations compound, or around Aryan Nations members.

Broadbent slowed his car, and pulled off on the shoulder of the road.

"Want to drive up and say hello to Butler?" Broadbent kidded.

"That's all right." Wassmuth laughed nervously.

"Place is looking pretty run down at the heel." Wassmuth commented on the sign at the end of road. The weather-beaten, rusted pole pitched forward as if getting ready to be sick, and black tape had been placed over the letters announcing the Wednesday evening service. Butler presently held only one service a week, Sunday morning at eleven.

"He draws five or six people to his services these days," Broadbent picked up.

"Good," Wassmuth offered, without rancor. "Any idea how many people live at the compound?"

"Near as we can tell just Butler and his wife, and the Tates."

Betty Tate continued to serve as Richard Butler's secretary; her husband did maintenance around the compound. Their son, David, was recently convicted of machine gunning one Missouri State Trooper to death, and gravely wounding another. Wassmuth considered it a tragedy that David Tate, not yet twenty years old, would spend the rest of his life in prison because of the ideology of hate with which he had been inculcated by his parents. Wassmuth thought that the senior Tates should have been tried along with their son.

"Most of the Aryans that moved into the area in the early eighties have moved away," Broadbent went on. "Those still here have taken on a low profile."

Wassmuth listened.

"The twenty-three Order convictions were the beginning of Butler's downfall," Broadbent recounted. "After the convictions of the two Order members for killing Alan Berg, Dorr and the Hawley's being charged with the bombings was a kick in the stomach to Butler. It turned the entire community against him."

"And now," Wassmuth mused, "the federal government is charging Butler, Miles and the ten other white supremacists with seditious conspiracy."

"I'd say we've heard the last of Richard Butler," Broadbent added.

"Hope you're right." Wassmuth turned his eyes away from the dirt road. "However, we said that after the State passed the Malicious Harassment Law. Butler has more lives than a barn full of cats."

"I'd be real surprised if he'll ever have the following he once had," Broadbent concluded.

"What hurt Butler and the Aryans was the attitude of the people around here," Wassmuth conjectured. "The citizens of north Idaho have undergone a real transformation about racial and religious issues."

Broadbent listened.

"All the seminars and education the Task Force sponsored has sensitized people to what happens to a community when the rights of even one person are trampled on," Wassmuth added. "When Butler first came up here, this was a fertile area for his white supremacist, hate ideology. I think the Task Force helped change that."

"This is a better place to live now," Broadbent answered.

Wassmuth looked across the seat at the stocky, bear of a man. "I'm ready to go anytime you are."

Broadbent eased his car out on the deserted road, and drove along the high, wooded meadowland toward the Interstate that would take them to Spokane.

"It's kind of funny," the Undersheriff said, as he steered the car, "that those people in New York are honoring us—a bunch of small town potato knockers—for what we've done for human rights. What possibly can we teach someone from such a huge and diversely-populated city as New York?"

"Maybe the scale of a city like Coeur d'Alene allows you to see things more clearly," Wassmuth conjectured. "Maybe we have a better sense of community than they do in New York... I don't know."

They drove in silence for a few minutes.

For the first time, really, Wassmuth allowed himself to take in the full implications of the honor they were to receive. The citizens of Coeur d'Alene were being recognized for their courage in standing up against hate; what the Task Force had done to counteract the racial crimes of the Aryan Nations was being held up as the model for other communities throughout the United States. Wassmuth felt like a long distance runner allowing himself to experience the sweet feeling of victory.

"You realize, Bill, that I've worked with you on the Task Force for nearly four years," Broadbent picked up, "and this is the first time I've ever seen you wear your Roman collar."

Wassmuth reached up and touched his clerical collar. A mischievously comical expression invaded his face. "You didn't know priests get better treatment on airplanes than you civilians do?"

Broadbent laughed. He reached into his shirt pocket, and withdrew a cigarette. "You mind?" he asked.

"Of course not." Wassmuth was the type of ex-smoker who did not mind others smoking, especially considering all the years he had blown smoke in the faces of others.

Broadbent cracked his window and lit up.

"There's a reason I haven't worn my collar up to now," Wassmuth began, more seriously. "I didn't want my work on the Task Force to be seen as a church issue. I wanted people to know I'm doing what I'm doing because it's the right thing to do, not just because it's the Christian thing to do."

They drove the rest of the way to the airport in silence. On the way, Wassmuth found himself thinking that Larry Broadbent was one of the most honest, decent and caring men he had ever known. He loved Broadbent, as he did Tony Stewart, Norm Gissel, Marshall Mend, and the other Task Force members. He found himself wondering why he did not feel as connected to his fellow clerics in the Idaho Roman Catholic Diocese as he did to his colleagues on the Human Rights Task Force.

THIRTY-ONE

Portland, Oregon

Portland is known for its green hills, active riverfront area and prosperous, tidy neighborhoods. A genteel and affluent city, it is spared many of the problems of its sister west coast cities, Los Angeles, San Francisco and Seattle. It rains often in Portland, much of the time mist or fog more than driving rain, a gentle moisture that falls against the plentiful vegetation like spray from a florist's aerator.

It was one of those heavy-misted nights when Ethiopian immigrant Mulugeta Seraw and two of his Ethiopian friends pulled to a stop in front of Seraw's apartment house.

The reed-thin, twenty-seven-year-old Seraw stepped from the car and turned to his friends. "Thanks for the ride," he said to the occupants of the car.

Two years in the United States, Seraw had a thick accent. He flashed his warm smile, and his dark eyes caught the glow from a nearby streetlight. "See you tomorrow."

"Okay," the driver answered, also with a heavy accent.

Seraw had turned for his house when another vehicle screeched to a halt next to his friend's car.

"What are *you* doin' around here, nigger?" one of the men in the car shouted. "This is white turf."

Seraw did not know who the man was calling to, and paid him no attention. He stepped towards his house without looking back.

Three men jumped from the car. Heads shaved, they wore cut-off jean jackets, and camouflage fatigue pants. One of the men had a large swastika stenciled on the back of his jacket. All three carried baseball bats.

"Who you walkin' away from, nigger?"

Seraw finally understood they were coming for him. He wheeled around in time to be struck across the bridge of his nose by the bat wielded by twenty-three-year-old Kenneth Mieske, whose street name was Ken Death. Seraw screamed with pain as he slumped to one knee. His eye glasses shattered, driving slivers of glass into his eyes.

Mieske and the two men with him, Steven Strasser and Kyle Hayden, were members of Eastside White Power, a Skinhead group with loose ties to the Aryan Nations and the Ku Klux Klan.

Meanwhile, Seraw's two friends piled out of the car. By the time they reached their friend, however, Seraw had been driven to the ground by a rain of blows.

"Stomp the nigger," nineteen-year-old Patricia Copp called from the Skinheads' car. "Spread his mongrel brains all over the grass."

Mieske wailed away on Seraw. The baseball bat striking the Ethiopian's head sounded like he was taking batting practice against a tree trunk. The other two Skinheads turned on Seraw's two friends. One of the Ethiopian men was driven backward by a blow to the face. The other was felled by a chopping blow to the side of the neck.

"Kill the niggers," the second woman in the car yelled, with hysterical glee.

Mieske drove the steel toes of his black Doc Marten work boots into Seraw's ribs, a sickening sound similar to beating dust out of a carpet.

"All right. Let's go," the tall, muscular Mieske ordered.

Strasser and Brewster, twenty and nineteen years old respectively, turned away from beating the other Ethiopians. The three Skinheads sprinted for their car. They jumped in, and, with a squeal of tires and roar of the engine, disappeared down the block.

One of Seraw's friends groaned and pushed to one knee. His friend also stirred; his nose was broken, and his face caked with blood and dirt.

"Who were those people?" the second man asked. "Why did they attack us?"

"I don't know," the other replied, massaging the side of his neck.

They moved slowly over to Seraw. His head was misshapen, and yellow, blood-traced mucous ran out of his mouth, nose and ears.

The one with the neck wound bent, and checked for a pulse. He moved his fingertips up and down on Seraw's neck, frantically searching for a sign of life. Not finding a pulse, he turned to his friend.

"Hurry," he said, panic invading his voice. "Find someone to call an ambulance."

The second man ran as fast as he could to the nearest house to summon help. He had an awful, sinking feeling that it was too late.

* * *

Located approximately 35 miles northwest of Seattle, Whidbey Island is one of the numerous islands that constitute the chain that lies within Puget Sound. Usually wet and dreary in December, the weather on the island had turned clear though chilly. The three parking lots at Whidbey Island State Park were uncharacteristically jammed with vehicles; generally this time of year there would be one or two cars in the lot, belonging to the hardiest of campers or hikers in search of outdoor solitude. So many people had driven out to Whidbey Island this Friday the authorities were forced to close the only road leading to the park. About thirty of the more than two hundred cars in the parking lots belonged to the group of Skinheads who had responded to the call by John Metzger, leader of the White Aryan Resistance Youth, to conduct a weekend vigil for slain Order leader, Robert Mathews. Mathews, a martyr and cult hero to white supremacists, died not far from the State Park four years earlier in a shoot-out with Federal Agents. The majority of vehicles in the parking areas, including three buses charted by United Front Against Fascism, belonged to anti-Nazi demonstrators here to protest the gathering of Skinheads. There was also the fleet of mobile TV news vans, cars belonging to reporters from newspapers in the northwest and as far away as New York, and over two dozen police cars. The police, along with park officials, were doing their best to keep Skinheads and protesters apart. It was such a potentially explosive situation, none of the reporters who had covered the upcoming event over the past few days had dared speculate what might happen if the vigil turned violent, for fear of provoking the confrontation.

So far, the authorities had managed to keep order. While the neo Nazis remained inside the park, the four hundred protesters—men, women and children, most carrying signs that stated things like,

"Nazis Go Home," and "Skinheads Aren't Welcome"—circled the entrance. News crews scurried about the parking lot, trying to identify and interview protest leaders and gather footage for evening report deadlines.

The protesters picked up a chant as they marched. "We beat the fear by being here. We beat the fear by being here."

TV camera crews closed in around a bearded man wearing a down vest.

"Why are you here?" one of the TV reporters barked.

"To express my concern over this gathering," Charlie James, a well-known community activist from Seattle answered. "The Skinheads are dangerous, hateful people, and their numbers are growing. So are the number of hate related crimes they commit against minorities."

A young woman stepped alongside James. She had long blond hair, finely sculpted features, and sad, searching blue eyes. She carried a sign that read, "You Are Next. Speak Out Against Bigotry."

"How about you?" a well-dressed female TV reporter asked the woman. "Why are you here?"

"I'm here to protest against bigotry, hatred and the killing" she answered. "The people inside the park conducting the vigil are hatemongers and racists, and we shouldn't tolerate them or their actions."

"A lot of people see them as laughable," a male reporter conjectured.

"That's exactly how people viewed the brownshirts in Germany in the 1920's, and the Klansmen of the 1930's," Charlie James answered, his face turning grave.

"There're a lot more of you than there are Skinheads inside the park," the female reporter picked up. "From what we're told there are only about 25 people camped in there."

"There will be more here tonight," the woman carrying the sign answered.

"Even one Skinhead is too many," the bearded man put in.

"Yeah," the woman added. "Even one Skinhead is a danger to decent, law-abiding citizens."

She and Charlie James rejoined the circle of marching protesters, who had picked up the chant, "Hey, hey, ho ho, Nazi bigots got to go."

Next the news teams closed in on Guerry Hodderson, National Secretary of the Freedom Socialist Party, and revolutionary socialist feminist organizer. Hodderson, wearing jeans, running shoes, and a flannel shirt, carried a sign that proclaimed, "Silence=Death."

"Why is the Freedom Socialist Party here?" a male reporter asked.

The woman with penetrating green eyes squared up with the newsman. "The FSP is an organization of people of color, Jews, gays and lesbians, unionists, the disabled—all of us Socialists. We know what the neo-Nazis have in mind for us: concentration camps, ovens, and gang-murder by storm troopers. None of us can stand by while others are picked off one by one. The Nazis won't just go away. We have to show them face to face that we're not afraid of them and are ready to fight."

"Why haven't you coordinated your efforts with some of the other human rights groups, like the Center for Democratic Renewal and the Northwest Coalition Against Malicious Harassment?" another reporter asked.

Hodderson grimaced. "Those two groups are the establishment and apologists. They conducted a low-key, candlelight vigil three nights before the Skinheads arrived. We chose to meet the Nazis head on."

"Aren't you afraid if you confront the Skinheads there will be violence?" asked another reporter. "Why not just let them meet and go away?"

"That's what Nazis count on," the woman answered. "They want to be left alone until they're strong enough to do real damage."

Hodderson turned and rejoined the protesters as they marched around the entrance to the park.

Over the next hour the reporters interviewed protesters. At one point a seventeen-year-old kid with closely cropped blond hair wandered up to the demonstration. It did not take the marchers long to spot the white supremacist button on his denim jacket. About 30 or 40 people quickly surrounded him, and began shouting, "Scum go home."

The youth sneered insolently. He was quickly escorted away by Charlie James, two police officers, and a park ranger, before the confrontation escalated.

The blond youth disappeared back into the campground. Within a few minutes, however, he returned accompanied by two other people. One was a middle-aged man with neatly combed brown hair, dressed in navy blue corduroy pants and a forest-green flannel shirt.

The third was a woman who looked to be in her late teens. Her head shaved, dressed in black, on her lapel was a button bearing the Nazi swastika.

TV news reporters quickly surrounded them. Police and park rangers immediately cordoned off the reporters and camera crew. Knots of protesters tried to ease past police, and chanted, "Scum go home."

"Who are you?" one of the reporters asked the clean-cut man.

"Karl Herler, from San Francisco," he responded with a calm smile. "I'm a member of the White Aryan Resistance."

The White Aryan Resistance had been founded by Tom Metzger. Metzger, a former Klansman, John Birch Society member, and candidate for Congress from Fallbrook, California, was expected to attend the Whidbey Island vigil. His son, John, founder of the White Aryan Resistance Youth, was also slated to join the Skinheads. Richard Butler was due later in the day.

"How many people are you expecting tonight?" someone asked.

"Nothing spectacular. Maybe a few dozen," the fifty-two year old Herler answered, quietly and politely. "This was not intended to be a mass rally."

"Why did you come?" one of the reporters asked.

"To honor Robert Mathews," Herler responded. His green eyes had a flinty hardness about them. "Robert Mathews was an American hero."

"Mathews was a bigoted, fascist hatemonger," one of the protesters tossed.

Herler ran a hand through his straight, gray-streaked blond hair.

"I think he was a martyr, a brave person who wanted to see a better, nice country."

"What is your connection to the Skinheads?" a male TV reporter asked.

"We're inspired by them; they breathe new life into us," Herler answered.

"What's your name?" someone asked the young woman in black.

"Karen," she answered. She wore fingerless gloves, a leather bandoleer adorned with silver studs diagonally across her chest, and in each ear several pierced earrings.

"You also came here to honor Robert Mathews?" a reporter asked.

"That's right," Karen answered, with a look of darting arrogance. "He stood up and died for what I believe in."

"And what's that?" someone asked.

"That race is the highest ideal."

"What does *that* mean?" another reporter asked, impatiently.

The young woman turned to him, and gave him a look that said he should know better than to ask such a dumb question.

"It means that the basis of what I believe is race and God," she said. "Ours is not a hate movement. We are superior. That's a fact."

"You damned wacko," someone called from the crowd of demonstrators. "Hatemongering, bigoted wacko. The whole bunch of ya."

The trio of white supremacists returned to the campground. The protesters resumed marching in a circle. They walked like that for several hours, before the three buses carrying the members of the

United Front Against Fascism left for Seattle. By late afternoon,
when Richard Butler arrived, less than fifty demonstrators remained.

The leader of the Aryan Nations stepped out of the passenger seat
of a black Buick. The driver was a whip-thin guy in his mid-thirties,
who wore the customary beret and form-fitting pale blue shirt with an
Aryan swastika on each shoulder.

Butler was dressed in a green V-neck sweater over a white shirt,
brown corduroy slacks, and tan thigh-length coat with a fur collar.
An Aryan swastika pin showed prominently on his sweater. The
remaining reporters recognized him immediately and closed in.

Butler faced the TV reporters, his hooded, reptilian eyes
betraying no emotion. He had come to dislike the press over the past
two years, as opposed to earlier in the decade when he spoke to any
reporter who ventured on to his Aryan Nations compound. Lately, he
had gone so far as to ban reporters from events staged at the
compound, claiming that their motives were to discredit him rather
than report news.

"Look," Butler began in his gravelly voice, "I have nothing to say
to you. I've come up here to lead a memorial service for Robert
Mathews, a true hero to his race."

A hush had fallen over the area. Even the remaining
demonstrators went strangely silent.

"What time is the service?" a reporter asked.

"Seven o'clock. At least that was what I was told," Butler
responded. His complexion was chalky, and his deeply lined skin
hung on his narrow face as if his skull had shrunk. He looked and
acted like a tired old man.

"How many people are expected to attend?"

"About fifteen or twenty," Butler answered, moving his eyes from reporter to reporter, as if attempting to get a fix on each one so he might recall their identity at a later date. "Again I can only go by what I've been told."

"You've publicly distanced yourself in the past from the activities of The Order," a reporter probed. "Why are you here to honor a man to whom you claim not to have been close?"

Butler's astonished expression indicated that if the guy was stupid enough to ask the question he would never understand the answer.

"Robert Mathews was a hero to the white race," Butler explained. "That is why I'm here. And the youth who have gathered here represent the future of the white race."

As if on cue, several Skinheads appeared out of the park, some with miniature American flags sewn next to swastikas on their jackets. They surrounded Butler and escorted the Aryan Nations leader into the park.

Another fifteen minutes passed, and White Aryan Resistance leader Tom Metzger arrived. Organizer of this vigil, Metzger had emerged over the past few years as a top white supremacist strategist. He was the driving force behind bringing the Skinheads into the white supremacist movement. Metzger also produced racist programs such as "Race and Reason", which aired on public access channels throughout the nation.

Metzger pushed hurriedly by the band of tired though eager reporters without saying a word. The round-faced, blond man, with the hairpiece that fooled no one, seemed intent on what lay ahead.

As the last of the news teams gathered up their equipment, one of the reporters said, "Don't you find all this a little scary? Skinheads assembling to honor Robert Mathews, head of a deadly, ruthless and violent group that was dedicated to overthrowing the government of the United States? Then Reverend Richard Butler shows up and calls the Skinheads the future of the white supremacist movement? These Skinheads get themselves a leader there could be hell to pay."

"Only if you're black or a Jew," another kidded.

"Or Hispanic, Asian, or anything but lily white," the first reporter finished.

THIRTY-TWO

Bill Wassmuth had been seeing Sam Stone for over a year, yet he still got the same unsettling feeling in his stomach before each of his weekly therapy sessions.

The door leading to the back office was pulled open. The tall and stout Stone stepped through the doorway, into the plain waiting room.

"Ready anytime you are, Bill," the therapist announced, in her calm and assured voice.

Wassmuth pushed out of the wooden captain's chair, and followed the woman back into her office. He sought out his familiar spot, the tan loveseat against the far wall.

Sam Stone sat in the armchair, facing him. She set her probing, gray eyes on him.

Wassmuth returned the gaze. He found the woman interesting. She wore her steel-gray-streaked brown hair short, which tended to call attention to her face with its pronounced bone structure and full strong lips.

"So?" she asked, the light from the nearby window dancing in her eyes, and a smile playing at her lips. "How are things going?"

"About the same," he answered.

"Could you be a bit more vague?" she asked, a twinkle in her eye.

"I'm fine," Wassmuth responded, knowing he was kidding himself. He had felt anything but fine over the past week since he had seen Sam Stone.

"Good," she answered, her quizzical look telling him she

understood he was playing for time. "Talk about fine."

He tugged at the collar of his blue, button-down shirt, and crossed and uncrossed his legs. He took a few deep breaths, and wondered what it was about this woman that enabled her to look right through him. In one sense, he was glad she could read him—it meant she was a good therapist—but it still made him uncomfortable.

"I don't know if I can do it any more," he began, the words surprising himself. Tears sprung to his eyes, and he got the feeling in his chest as if his insides were being scraped by one of those instruments the dentist used to removed the plaque from his teeth.

"Do what any more?" she asked. She reached out and straightened the crease of her charcoal-brown wool pleated slacks.

"I don't think I want to live the rest of my life alone," Wassmuth added, giving words to the realization that had grown inside him over the past months he had been seeing Sam Stone.

Sam Stone waited, letting him sit with the feelings that accompanied the statement.

Not wishing to spend the rest of his life alone was an idea that had been forming since he realized during one of his early sessions with Sam Stone that he was an alcoholic, and nothing he did seemed to be able to rein in his drinking. After that session, he quit drinking. Once he stopped anesthetizing himself with alcohol he began questioning whether he wanted to live what remained of his life alone and celibate.

Still, the prospect of resigning as pastor of St. Pius X Church nearly paralyzed him. Being a priest was all Bill Wassmuth had ever wanted to do, or ever had done. Every bit of training and sacrifice he had done as a child had been to prepare himself to enter the seminary and become a priest. Later, when people asked him why he chose the clergy as a profession, Wassmuth replied that there were only two options for a young man in Greencreek, Idaho: either you got married, or went into the seminary. Since he was related to most of the people in his hometown, he reasoned, and it was not cool to marry a cousin, he went into the priesthood. Actually the lack of female prospects in his hometown had nothing to do with it. As a young man, Wassmuth never considered himself the marrying type. He did not dislike girls, nor was he gay; he simply never considered anything other than being a priest.

Which was why these new and powerful feelings he had been experiencing for the several months had taken him by surprise. What had begun as a dull, distant stirring turned into something he likened to being constantly hungry. He did everything in his power to make the feeling go away. He prayed about it. He upped the number of miles he jogged each day. Nothing worked, not even the intensity of his work with the Task Force, or the demands of his pastoral duties.

"You were saying that you didn't know whether you wanted to spend the rest of your life alone," Sam Stone said, bringing him out of his head, where he retreated to escape the intensity of the feelings he was experiencing.

"That's right."

"Have you met someone?"

"Not really. I've been attracted to women, though I've been careful to honor my pledge of celibacy. No, it's something else. I guess I can't say it any simpler than I've just had this realization that I don't want to spend the rest of my life by myself."

"How do you see your life today?"

"I feel a sense of completion about things," he added, working hard to keep his emotions down. "The parish is doing well; the new building is done, and the congregation is very strong and healthy."

Wassmuth paused, and reached for a tissue from the box on the maple coffee table. He blotted the pools of tears under his eyes.

"The Task Force is up and running," he picked up. "And, despite Butler and the other white supremacists being acquitted of charges of seditious conspiracy in the Arkansas trial, the Aryan Nations movement is in disarray. Their membership is on the decline, and Butler and his group haven't caused any trouble since the bombings."

Privately, Wassmuth was outraged that Butler and the others were acquitted by an all-white jury in a southern state, though he was careful to state publicly that he believed in the justice system and would abide by the verdict.

"Beyond that, there's the new law we worked hard on getting through the legislature that forbids the Aryans or anyone from conducting paramilitary training. And the other one that gives victims of harassment the right to sue for civil remedy," Wassmuth completed. "It seems as though my work here is finished."

"Sounds like you've made your decision."

"Maybe it's been made for me," Wassmuth said, and smiled. "No place to go but down from here."

She chuckled with understanding. Wassmuth had recently been named "Citizen of the Year" by the largest newspaper in the state, *The Idaho Statesman*. The award was heady stuff for a parish priest, and a major public relations coup for the Kootenai County Task Force.

"Have you given any thought about what you would do?" the therapist asked.

"It'd probably be best if after resigning from my parish I move away."

"Really?" she asked.

"People here would always expect me to act like Father Bill Wassmuth. They'd have a lot of trouble accepting me as just plain Bill, private citizen, you know, a sexual being." His face turned red. He had never referred to himself that way before, and it embarrassed him. "I'm afraid they'd make me a hostage to whom I've been in the past, and never allow me to be who I'm becoming."

"Makes sense to me." Sam Stone shifted in her chair. "Where would you go?"

"Maybe Seattle. I've always liked it there. It would be appropriate that the Northwest Coalition Against Malicious Harassment be headquartered there."

Wassmuth had been elected president of the recently formed five state Northwest Coalition Against Malicious Harassment. The human rights organization consisted of more than 200 organizations located within Washington, Oregon, Idaho, Montana and Wyoming. It was a coalition of human rights groups whose aim was to apply the principles of the Kootenai County Task Force on Human Relations to communities throughout the northwest, a dream come true for Wassmuth.

"How long have you been a priest, Bill?"

"Twenty-one years."

"You thought about what it will be like not being one?"

Wassmuth felt somehow irritated by the comment. "I won't resign from the priesthood, just as pastor of St. Pius."

"What if you get married?"

"I'll leave that decision up to the Church," he said, resolutely. "Maybe one day they'll wake up, and allow priests to marry."

"When will you leave your parish?"

"I figure it'll take me about six months to tie up all the loose ends." Wassmuth's mouth moved into a smile. "Another hour or so to pack... One of the virtues of living a life of voluntary poverty— everything I own fits into my car. And it's a compact!"

* * *

Six months after his session with Sam Stone, Bill Wassmuth stunned his congregation by announcing at Sunday morning Mass that he was resigning as pastor of St. Pius X parish. He explained to the packed church that he was moving to Seattle.

The parishioners of St. Pius X expressed their gratitude for his service to them by taking up a collection and presenting Wassmuth with a check for five thousand dollars. This was far better than he fared with his diocese. After twenty-one years of service as a priest, all of it served in the Idaho diocese, Wassmuth was given a month's salary—five hundred dollars—by Bishop Sylvester Trienan. Along with this severance pay, Wassmuth was notified by the Bishop that because he decided to leave the priesthood he would lose his vested interest in the Diocesan retirement plan. This presented Wassmuth with a certain bitter irony; he was one of the church leaders who some years back drafted the retirement plan for church employees, including priests.

Twenty-one years with one firm, Wassmuth mused sadly, and all he had to show for it was five hundred dollars. However, as it often is with those who come to know the exhilaration of freedom after some period of physical or spiritual bondage, Bill Wassmuth was too excited about what lay ahead to grieve the loss of his retirement benefits.

His main regret about leaving Coeur d'Alene, beyond losing contact with the members of his congregation, was resigning as spokesperson of the Task Force. He felt more spiritually aligned with Marshall Mend, Tony Stewart, Norm Gissel, Ginny DeLong and the others than he had with his fellow priests in the Idaho Diocese. The feeling he had for his friends on the Task Force was like he imagined combat buddies felt about one another. And what went on in north Idaho for almost a decade had been like a war.

Wassmuth's sense of loss at leaving the Task Force was softened somewhat by the knowledge that he would be working with Tony Stewart, and, in some measure, the other members as president of the Northwest Coalition.

So, on a hot, still July day, an anxious, fearful and excited Bill Wassmuth packed everything he owned into his Mercury Topaz, and drove to Seattle to start a new life.

EPILOGUE

The convictions of members of the Order and Aryan Republican Army and others associated with the Aryan Nations, and large court settlements against the Klan and other right wing extremist groups, caused a brief lull in the growth of hate groups. Currently, however, neo-Nazi, Christian Patriot and Christian Identity groups are once again gaining in membership and strength throughout Idaho and the rest of the United States. The Southern Poverty Law Center Of Montgomery, Alabama estimates that the year 1998 saw the number of hate groups in the U.S. exceed five hundred. One such white supremacist organization, The World Church of the Creator, has mushroomed from eight chapters in 1995 to forty-six in 1999. The World Church of the Creator listed among its members Benjamin Nathaniel Smith, who, on July 4, 1999, randomly gunned down nearly a dozen black, Jewish and Asian people in Illinois and Indiana. Another group that operates on the edges of the racist moment, the Council of Conservative Citizens, counts some fifteen thousand members in twenty-two states, and has enjoyed the flirtations of such politicians as Senator Trent Lott (R-Miss.), U.S. Representative Bob Barr (R-Ga.), and Mississippi Governor Kirk Fordice. Lawrence Russell Brewer, one of the three men who dragged James Byrd Jr. to death behind their pickup truck in Texas, was reported to tell his companions that "we're starting The Turner Diaries early." And, according to the Southern Poverty Law Center, "there has been a rise in the number of far-right extremists implicated in drug-dealing to raise money for (their) movement."

Richard Butler has emerged as patriarch of white supremacist hate groups. He is also considered a master strategist by both his sympathizers and law enforcement. After a period in which he was openly hostile to the media, Butler returned to his strategy of manipulating the press, gaining him national and international recognition. He has also broadened his appeal with statements like "Left-wing multiculturalism is being forced down our throats." Closely related to Hitler's Minister of Propaganda Josef Goebbel's proclamation of, "When I hear the word culture, I reach for my revolver," such inflammable rhetoric has aligned Butler's ideology with that of more established, accepted organizations such as the NRA, English-only groups, the right-to-life movement, various militia groups, and anti-immigration organizations. By broadening their message, right-wing extremists have earned the advocacy of certain local and national politicians. This includes, according to the May 8, 1995 issue of *Time* magazine, the staunch support of two Republicans in Congress, Helen Chenoweth of Idaho, and Steve Stockman of Texas.

Over the past several years Butler has drawn numerous high profile white supremacists as well as rank-and-file, right wing extremists to Idaho to help realize the Aryan chief's plan for an all-white homeland. Among those have been Randy Weaver, John Trochmann, and James 'Bo' Gritz—the much-decorated Vietnam veteran, and 1992 presidential candidate of the Populist Party. Gritz purchased 280 acres of land near Grangeville, Idaho, on which he is creating Almost Heaven, a homeland for his Christian Covenant Community, a decidedly white supremacist organization whose members receive paramilitary training. Louis Beam, former KKK leader and white supremacist implicated in the attack on Vietnamese-American fishermen in Galveston Bay, also moved for a time to north Idaho. Beam's oratorical skills, and organizational and computer abilities helped the Aryan Nations locate chapters in 18 states throughout the U.S. Gerald 'Jack' McLamb, former Phoenix, Arizona police officer and Christian Patriot, has joined Bo Gritz at Almost Heaven. Lamb holds that law enforcement personnel must fight against elected leaders rather than enforce the laws. Paul Hall, editor of the nationally distributed anti-Semitic newspaper, *The Jubilee*, has also purchased property near Hayden Lake. Mark Furhman, racist ex-cop from Los Angeles who gained notoriety in the O.J. Simpson trial, has relocated to north Idaho. Buford Furrow was an active participant at the Hayden Lake compound before turning his guns on children at a Southern California Jewish Youth Center and killing an Asian-American mail carrier.

Several recent events have galvanized the will of the Aryan Nations, militia groups and other white supremacists groups, not only in the northwest, but throughout the United States. These have been portrayed by most far right publications, including *American's Bulletin*, as an outgrowth of an escalating government conspiracy against far right Christians because of their religious beliefs, and an eventual usurping of the rights of all white Americans. Some of these incidents are the shoot-out between avowed white supremacist Randy Weaver and Federal Marshals in Ruby Ridge, Idaho, the standoff between U.S. Marshals and the Montana Freemen, and the deadly confrontation between the Branch Davidians and the Bureau of Alcohol and Firearms officers in Waco, Texas. The Weaver incident was given as the motivation for Darwin Michael Gray's plan to blow up the federal building in Spokane. Gray, a friend of Kevin Harris (participant in the shoot-out against federal officers at Ruby Ridge), and an affiliate of the Aryan Nations, was arrested with material to construct a fertilizer bomb and blueprints for the Spokane federal building.

The Montana Militia standoff has become a rallying cry for the Christian Patriots as an example of "the ZOG government crushing a movement of American patriots."

The Branch Davidian siege was offered as the main motivation of Timothy McVeigh and Terry Nichols for the terrorist bombing of the federal building in Oklahoma City, Oklahoma. McVeigh and Nichols were incensed at the government's handling of the Waco affair, and held federal officials accountable for the many deaths at the Branch Davidian compound. The two men were highly influenced by the novel, *The Turner Diaries*, which chronicles a group of armed militants that overthrow the Jewish-controlled U.S. government to restore America to its rightful heirs, white Christian people. An avowed disciple of the book, McVeigh, while in the military, circulated *The Turner Diaries* to other enlisted men. Once discharged, he traveled the gun show circuit selling the book and promoting its ideas to whoever would listen.

Richard Butler is also a fan of *The Turner Diaries*. The book's author, William Pierce, has been a frequent visitor to the Aryan compound at Hayden Lake. Pierce's words of hate and division echo Butler's.

Richard Butler, Bo Gritz, Louis Beam, Randy Weaver, John Trochmann, William Pierce, Timothy McVeigh, Benjamin Nathaniel Smith, all names linked together by the common strands of race hatred and a boundless and seething paranoia over the power of the U.S. Government.

Butler and his minions no longer operate in a vacuum in north Idaho, however. Due in large part to the Kootenai County Task Force on Human Right's education program, the area's citizens—including some who once resisted the Task Force's work—for the most part speak in one voice for the rights of all. Further, the city administration is attempting to implement laws requiring damage deposit and fees to cover costs resulting from parades and marches, specifically those hate groups like the Aryan Nations. A major part of the funding to research the constitutionality of these laws was provided by businessman, Duane Hagadone, an early critic of the Task Force.

The Task Force and national human rights groups are closely monitoring the Aryans' actions. An example is the January 25, 1999 civil lawsuit filed against Richard Butler on behalf of a mother and her son who were the targets of a shooting attack on a public road outside the Aryan compound. The suit was filed by Coeur d'Alene attorney Norm Gissel and Morris Dees of the Southern Poverty Law Center.

Another indication that the Aryan Nations' influence in north Idaho is waning was the Aryan march in Coeur d'Alene on July 18,

1998. Butler was only able to muster ninety faithful to march, while approximately five hundred counterdemonstrators lined the parade route. On that same day, another eight hundred people participated in a nearby Human Rights Celebration. A repeat march on July 10th drew only twenty white supremacists, who were again faced by hundreds of protesters.

Still, Butler and fellow north Idaho white supremacists influence a growing national network of hatemongers throughout the U.S. A January 1999 Los Angeles Times article states, "*Klanwatch*, which monitors hate groups, in a recent profile called Butler 'the hub of the wheel of racist revolution, the eye of the white supremacist storm.' The future of the movement he founded, the profile goes on to say, 'may shape the future of the extremist right.' From Hayden Lake (Butler's Aryan Nations) operates one of the most active distribution networks in the country for racist and fascist literature, and oversees campaigns to organize both convicts and guards at prisons throughout the country."

Butler has recently been the recipient of significant financial support from two wealthy northern California businessmen. Carl E. Story and R. Vincent Bertollini, highly successful players in the Silicon Valley computer industry, claim they have fifteen million dollars to invest in Butler's Christian Identity movement. Both Story and Bertollini state they are ardent believers of Butler's white separatist ideology.

Whether the Aryan Nations headquarters continues to be located in Hayden Lake, Idaho or is moved elsewhere, it appears Butler's work of promoting hate and division and violence will go on. Butler has financial backing, and, at eighty-one years old, is still active. He continues to provide the inspiration for younger followers who have the energy to put hate into action. He has also apparently selected a successor in Neumann Britton. Britton, married to the widow of Gordon Kahl—Posse Comitatus leader who killed two U.S. marshals in 1983 and was later gunned down in an Arkansas shoot-out—mirrors Butler's ideology of hate, and bears an uncanny resemblance to the older Richard Butler.

Not everyone in white supremacist groups commits violent acts; but violence frequently springs out of such groups. Moreover, the presence of such groups can intimidate whole communities unless voices for justice and respect are raised to counter words of hate. To ignore hate groups, even though they usually include relatively small numbers of people, is to miscalculate the impact that they can have on a community, and to miss an opportunity to bring a community together to take another step toward justice for all.

Bill Wassmuth

AFTERWORD

The reader may wish to know the present whereabouts and circumstances of the principal characters in this book.

Bill Wassmuth completed a decade as Executive Director of the Northwest Coalition Against Malicious Harassment in 1999. He lectures and speaks widely on the subjects of human rights, extremism and white supremacy. He was married on July 1, 1989.

Wassmuth was the recipient of the Alan Gleitsman Foundation Award For People Who Make A Difference in 1992, the National Education Association Martin Luther King, Jr. Memorial Award in 1993, and the American Civil Liberties Union William O. Douglas Award in 1999.

Larry Broadbent lost his job as Kootenai County Undersheriff when his superior, Sheriff Merf Stalder, was defeated in his re-election bid in the November 1988 general election. Broadbent attended college to obtain a degree in Criminal Justice. He retired from law enforcement, and passed away in 1995.

Marshall Mend continues to serve on the Kootenai County Task Force on Human Relations. Mend convinced the Idaho State Association of Realtors to adopt the `Idaho Is For Everyone' logo as its official trademark. The logo depicts faces of people of all races, and presently appears on Idaho State Association of Realtors' printed matter.

Mend's real estate business continues to prosper, as, once again, people are moving into the Coeur d'Alene area.

Richard Butler still operates out of his Aryan Nations compound in Hayden Lake. In addition to his 'ministerial' duties, he publishes his newsletter, and coordinates information among the various white supremacist organizations throughout the United States and Canada. Butler has also been working hard to bring the various Skinhead splinter groups under the umbrella of the Aryan Nations.

A victim of cardiovascular disease, Butler underwent open heart surgery. The cardiologist who performed the surgery is Jewish, and the operating nurse is black.

Tony Stewart teaches Political Science at North Idaho College. He is past president of the Northwest Coalition Against Malicious Harassment, and continues as a leader of the Kootenai County Task Force on Human Relations. In addition, he hosts and produces the 'Public Forum,' a continuing series on social issues that appears weekly on public television. Tony is tireless in presenting seminars to the people of north Idaho, including the highly successful Martin Luther King, Jr. Day celebration, the largest of its kind in Idaho.

Norm Gissel continues as a board member of the Kootenai County Task Force on Human Relations. He has a private law practice in Coeur d'Alene.

Ginny DeLong coordinates the Peace Camp for Youth for the Kootenai County Task Force on Human Relations.

Skip Kuck is involved with several human rights task forces in north Idaho, and is an active member of the Board of Directors of the Northwest Coalition Against Malicious Harassment.

The Task Force and the community of Coeur d'Alene are endeavoring to guarantee the basic human rights of every citizen of north Idaho. The people involved in that effort are too numerous to mention here.

In 1991 the Task Force released a 90 minute documentary film titled, Stand Up To Hate Groups By Saying Yes To Human Rights.

Rick Morse is minister of Lake Washington Christian Church Disciples of Christ in Kirkland, Washington, and is active in human rights work in the Seattle area.

Dina Tanners lives in Spokane, and continues her human rights work through Gonzaga University and her synagogue.

Tom Metzger emerged as mentor to many neo-Nazi Skinhead groups across the country. However, in 1990, Metzger, his son, John, and the White Aryan Resistance organization they lead, lost a civil suit filed by the Southern Poverty Law Center on behalf of the family of Mulugeta Seraw. Tom Metzger was ordered to pay five million dollars in damages, John Metzger, one million, and the White Aryan Resistance organization, three million dollars. With the verdict, the Metzgers lost their influence in the white supremacist movement, particularly among neo-Nazi Skinheads.

Kenneth Mieske (Ken Death) and Kyle Hayden were convicted of murder, aggravated assault with intent to kill, and racial intimidation, in the killing of Mulugeta Seraw and the beating of his two companions. **Steven Strasser**, the third Skinhead involved on the attack of the trio of Ethiopians in Portland, was convicted of assault and racial intimidation. All three are currently serving prison sentences in Oregon.

Patricia Copp, one of the two women in the Skinheads' car the night of the fatal attack on Mulugeta Seraw, and who cheered Ken Mieske as he beat Seraw to death with the baseball bat, was interviewed on Portland television about the attack. She did not understand what the big deal was. After all, she said, Seraw was only a "nigger."

To order additional copies of *Hate Is My Neighbor*

_____ copies @ $14.95   _____

shipping and handling @ $1.50 per copy   _____

                        Total   _____

Send this form, along with check or money order to:

Stand Together Publishers
P.O. Box 425
Ellensburg, WA 98926-0425